William Garden Blaikie, Thomas Guthrie

Saving Knowledge

Addressed to young men

William Garden Blaikie, Thomas Guthrie

Saving Knowledge

Addressed to young men

ISBN/EAN: 9783337248208

Printed in Europe, USA, Canada, Australia, Japan

Cover: Foto ©Paul-Georg Meister /pixelio.de

More available books at **www.hansebooks.com**

SAVING KNOWLEDGE

SAVING KNOWLEDGE

Addressed to Young Men

By THOS. GUTHRIE, D.D. AND W. G. BLAIKIE, D.D.

STRAHAN & CO., PUBLISHERS
56 LUDGATE HILL, LONDON
1870

NOTE.

CIRCUMSTANCES having made it necessary to divide the authorship of the following papers, it may be right to say that the 3rd, 4th, 7th, 8th, and 11th are by DR GUTHRIE, and the other chapters by DR BLAIKIE.

CONTENTS.

CHAP.		PAGE
I.	GOD'S VERDICT ON MAN	1
II.	GOD'S SENTENCE ON MAN	24
III.	THE EVIL OF SIN	50
IV.	MAN'S INABILITY TO SAVE HIMSELF	75
V.	GOD'S GIFT TO MAN	101
VI.	THE SAVIOUR'S PERSON	125
VII.	THE WORK AND GLORY OF THE SAVIOUR	147
VIII.	THE WAY OF SALVATION	171
IX.	THE SINNER'S LINK TO THE SAVIOUR—FAITH	202
X.	THE SPIRIT OF LIFE	227
XI.	MADE HOLY	255
XII.	THE SACRAMENTS	319

I.

GOD'S VERDICT ON MAN.

CHRISTIANITY bears, on its very face, to be a grand scheme of restoration. It professes to deal with a ruined being, and its object is to recover him from ruin. It is not a mere hot-house, where warmth and shelter are given to tender plants, enabling them to thrive and become beautiful, when the open air would stunt or kill them. It is not a mere auxiliary force, added to the moral powers of man, like a screw power in a feeble sailing vessel, to enable him to get on faster and farther than he otherwise would. It is not a mere system of decoration, giving a beautiful finish to a course of improvement which education, and civilization, and culture, have advanced a long way. It embraces all these objects among its subordinate aims, but they are not of its essence, they are not what it claims to be. It is common, in these times, to speak favourably of Christianity as a most valuable hot-house, a most useful propeller, a charming decorator. Such compliments are often accompanied with sneers at the idea of its being much more, or of man's needing much more. But any view of Christianity must fall infinitely short of the truth, and in practice prove most pernicious, that does not take account of its main claim and profession—as a divine provision for the removal of man's guilt, and for the restoration of life, purity, and beauty to his deformed and fallen nature.

The very name given to the founder of Christianity by the angel of the Lord, implied that this was its essential purpose. He was not to bear a name indicating a great Reformer merely, or a great Teacher, or a great Priest, or a great King, but one combining all these offices, in their furthest reach and deepest meaning—'Thou shalt call his name Saviour, for he shall save his people from their sins.' He did not come merely to teach, or to civilize, or to rule, or to reform, but to save. He refused to allow his gift to man to be described by any term short of Life, in the highest meaning of that word, or to accept the homage of those who would not believe that life could be had only through vital fellowship with Him. (John vi. 30.) He welcomed the shouts of the multitude when they called out 'Hosanna,' ascribing to Him, in that very word, the power to save. He felt it no shame, as He hung on the cross, to have the word 'JESUS' inscribed over His head. Indeed it was to place His claim to that name on an unchallengeable basis, that He bore the cross and its cursed death. And, after His ascension, His apostles showed how truly they apprehended the grand purpose of His incarnation and death by their use of the word salvation. It became a consecrated word. 'Neither is there SALVATION in any other; for there is no other name given under heaven among men whereby we must be SAVED.' All other applications of the word are dwarfed and overshadowed by the meaning it bears in connection with Christ. No doubt, in a sense, a man rescued from shipwreck, is saved. A child snatched from off the rails just as an express train is dashing along, is saved. A bedrid paralytic rescued from a burning house, is saved. A young man dragged from the meshes of intemperance, is saved. But in every one of these instances, who does not feel that it is but a mere fraction of the force of the great word that is put forth; and that its measureless compass of meaning is conveyed only when it is said of the sinner, pardoned, purified, and blessed by Jesus Christ, that once lost, now he is SAVED?

There are strange stories of little children stolen in infancy by gipsies from the happy homes of their parents, retaining in after years a vague impression of the condition from which they were torn. No recollection was distinct enough to be shaped into definite form; but a misty notion of a happier time floated like a thin vapour through their brain. A similar impression of an unfallen state seems to have retained its hold on the human race. There is an instinctive feeling in us that we are not what once we were; that the early days of our race were happier and brighter, that the golden age of innocence and bliss has degenerated, till at last our lot has fallen upon the age of iron. Alongside of this feeling lies our instinctive hope of better days to come, the longing for a paradise regained, out of which poetry is constantly forming so many pictures of peace and beauty. Such fancies are vague, and they are apt to deceive. They may nourish the feeling that this fall is a pure misfortune, a sad evil for which no one of us is more responsible than the babe unborn. At all events, we need a more sure word of prophecy. What *is* this fallen state in which we are? How came we to be in it? What are its bearings and consequences? And how may we escape from it? The word of God professes to be given for the very purpose of answering these questions; if it be so, the more closely we keep to its guidance, the more accurately shall we be informed, both of the nature of our ruin, and of the mode of recovery which has been provided by Christ.

Hardly have we opened the Bible, and begun our inquiry, when our attention is arrested by the perpetual occurrence of the words 'sin' and 'sinner.' They swarm in every page. And alongside of them we find hosts of synonymous words—transgression, trespass, iniquity, unrighteousness, ungodliness, rebellion, uncleanness, corruption, guilt. And what is strange, there is not a great deal in the Bible about misfortune or calamity. The leading impression conveyed is not, that through some cause over which he had no control, man has come to be what he now is. He is not represented as the innocent victim of misfortune. His case is a far more serious one in the eyes of his God. He is a criminal. That, undoubtedly, is the outstanding consideration by which the Bible accounts for the state of man.

It is this that gives such an aspect of gloom to his whole history, as traced in the Bible. It is this, too, that makes the problem of his redemption so difficult. If man's condition were the result mainly of misfortune, or of weakness, or of imperfection, or of exposure to fierce and noxious influences, there could be no great difficulty in remedying it. It is because he is a SINNER that the case is so serious and the difficulty so great. And it is because Jesus Christ has surmounted this difficulty, and has made complete provision for every feature and aspect of man's sinful state, that his salvation is so glorious, and the security of all who are united to him so unchallengeably complete.

The charge of the Bible against man as a sinner is made in many different forms. Thus, in the first place, there are passages not a few in which the whole race, without exception, is brought in 'guilty' before God. 'There is none righteous, no not one.' 'The imagination of man's heart is evil from his youth.' 'God made man upright, but they have sought out many inventions.' 'If thou, Lord, shouldest mark iniquities, O Lord, who shall stand?' 'All have sinned, and come short of the glory of God.' 'If we say that we are without sin, we deceive ourselves, and the truth is not in us.' 'In many things, we offend all.' Nothing can be wider or more unrestricted than such statements as these. And lest any doubt should remain as to their bearing, some of them are deliberately brought together in the third chapter of the Epistle to the Romans, and the very purpose and end of them is solemnly declared to be to establish a verdict of guilty against the whole race of man, 'that every mouth may be stopped, and all the world become guilty before God.'

Not less emphatic is the testimony of Scripture to the continued depravity of individuals and of communities that have enjoyed very special advantages, and have had all the resources of Divine care and nurture lavished upon them. A tree bearing bitter fruit in a wild and uncultivated desert is very likely a bad tree, but if it bear the same bitter fruit in a garden, with all the advantages of climate, soil, and cultivation, the proof of its badness is more decisive and complete. If we compare the barbarian and the Scythian to the tree in the desert, the seed of Abraham will correspond to the tree in the sheltered and cultivated garden. To them every conceivable advantage and encouragement was given, and the great vine-dressser could appeal to themselves in proof of His exhaustive attention. 'What could have been done more to my vineyard that I have not done in it? Wherefore, when I looked that it should bring forth grapes, brought it forth wild grapes?'

Equally clear, and in some respects even more impressive, are the countless passages in which the holiest of men are found to deplore their depravity, confessing that in their flesh, or natural state, dwelt no good thing, and that it was by the grace of God alone they were what they were. Such confessions derive singular depth and earnestness from the fact that the spiritual vision of God vouchsafed to these men exalted immeasureably their ideas of purity on the one hand, and deepened their horror of sin on the other. Job, perfect and upright though he was, according to the common standard of men, no sooner comes into the Divine presence than he sees himself covered with impurity: 'I have heard of thee by the hearing of the ear, but now mine eye seeth thee; wherefore I abhor myself, and repent in dust and ashes.' In that dread presence where the voices of seraphim cry 'Holy, holy, holy!' Isaiah is overwhelmed with the sense of his uncleanness: 'Woe is me,' he cries, 'for I am undone! for I am a man of unclean lips, and I dwell in the midst of a people of unclean lips; for mine eyes have seen the King, the Lord of hosts.' King David, after his terrible declension, is horror-stricken when he enters the presence of God: his sin glares on him like a fiend, and he can see nothing in himself but wickedness: 'Behold, I was shapen in iniquity, and in sin did my mother conceive me.' St Paul, when he looks into the perfect law of God, not only perceives a sad contrast between what he is and what he should be, but finds a horrible law of corruption roused by the very contact into such overwhelming activity as to extort the cry, 'O wretched man that I am! who shall deliver me from the body of this death?' And there is no part of the experience of Bible saints which honest believers, in all ages of the world, have felt more true of themselves. Whatever differences there may be in the experience of good men, all agree in this, that sin is engrained, so to speak, in the very substance of their nature—that an awful attraction, as strong as the gravitation of the earth, drags them to evil, and that even their life-long struggles against sin leave them in so unsatisfactory a state, that their only hope of final acceptance lies in the merit of the Saviour, and their only prospect of becoming meet for heaven in the promised and all-sufficient grace of the Holy Ghost.

Such passages and such testimonies furnish the clearest proof that in the sight of God all men are sinners. Let us now try to analyze this depravity somewhat—to resolve it into some of its constituent elements, and bring it home, as a sad reality, to the heart and conscience of all. The two great centres of the alleged depravity of man are UNGODLINESS and SELFISHNESS—the one having reference to his relation to God, the other mainly to his relation to his fellow-men.

1. UNGODLINESS. The great charge of the Bible against man is that he is regardless of God. In his heart he fails in every feeling, and in his life he comes short of every service, which is due by him to such a Being. Consider, for example, how sadly he fails in the *inward esteem or reverence* which he owes to God. God is the perfection of beauty and excellence; every quality worthy of our regard exists in Him in infinite fulness. All other beauty and all other excellence are but feeble sparks from the great source

of beauty and excellence. The wisdom of a Newton, the benevolence of a Howard, the tenderness of a Ruth, the generosity of a Joseph, the friendship of a Jonathan, are but stray and feeble rays from the One great Sun—the all-glorious and unchangeable God. Yet, how dead are all men's hearts to this beauty and excellence! When I look at a rainbow, or a lovely sunset, the sense of beauty fills my mind; when, stricken with conscious meanness, I experience the generosity of a friend; or when I follow a self-denying philanthropist through scenes of sickening vice and misery, and witness his untiring love; or when I read of noble-hearted men and women risking their lives to rescue shipwrecked seamen, my heart swells, my bosom heaves: but when I think of God, I am dull, languid, lifeless; I dismiss the thought as ungenial; it has no sunshine for my heart. Consider God in any of the relations in which He stands to us, and how miserably defective are our feelings! Our Creator and Preserver, how well is He entitled to our reverence and gratitude—yet how independently we carry ourselves towards Him! Our Owner and Master, what a claim He has to our service—yet how disposed are we ever to say, 'Our lips are our own, who is Lord over us?' Our King, our Lawgiver, and our Judge, on whose will and pleasure our everlasting destinies hang,—how little we think of pleasing Him! Our God and Father, who longs for our affections, who throws all divine earnestness into the request, 'My son, give me thy heart,' and whom one genuine look of love from us would gladden infinitely more than the first smiles of her gentle infant gladden the doting mother,—how coldly and heedlessly we leave Him to say, 'If I be a Father, where is mine honour? and if I be a Master, where is my fear?' How strange and sad it is to find God contrasting the mindfulness of the very beasts with the regardlessness of man! Pointing to the ox that knows his owner, and the ass his master's crib,—pointing to the stork of heaven that knows his appointed time, and the turtle and the crane and swallow, that observe the time of their coming, and deploring, in contrast to these, that 'Israel doth not know, my people doth not consider!' Contrasting the fidelity of the sons of Jonadab, who would have died rather than forget their father's charge, with the heedlessness of those whom he had nourished and brought up as children! Contrasting the attachment of the very heathen to their idol-gods, and the constancy with which they continued to honour them, with the changing fickleness of the professed children of Jehovah!

How strange, too, that it should be so difficult to convince men of this great habit of sin! That they should so seldom think that anything is seriously wrong, when the heart is thus dead to God, and that they should be so little shocked, either at themselves or at the world at large, though virtually they are trying to dethrone God, and govern things not after His fashion, but their own! It is not necessary to prove men murderers, or adulterers, or blasphemers, or revellers, to bring them in guilty before God. It is enough that their lives have been spent in regardlessness of Him, as if no such Being lived, or as if He had nothing to do with them, or they with Him. The sense of unworthiness that comes over one when he awakes to a sense of the virtual atheism of his past life, is in no sensible degree impaired by the consideration that outwardly his life may have been blameless, and that his relations to his fellow-men may have been amiable and kind. It is the discovery of his godlessness that distresses him; the thought that all his life long he has been neglecting the God in whom he lives and moves and has his being; that in place of the regard due to his Creator, the submission due to his Sovereign, the reverence due to his God, the affection due to his Father, and the gratitude, confidence, and devotion due to his Redeemer, his heart has presented an absolute blank—an utter void of every living sentiment suitable to his relation to the Most High! How can it be supposed that he has fulfilled the great ends of his being, when absolute death has reigned in the region that should have been alive with the warmest feelings and the most spontaneous activities? A soul dead to God, how is it conceivable that God should be pleased with such a phenomenon? So far from being astonished that he should be declared guilty before God, the wonder is that God should not long ago have put an end to a life so unprofitable. He feels himself so utterly unworthy, that Divine grace alone can effect his salvation; and while he lives on earth, he can never cease to mourn the godless tendencies that still remain in him, nor to feel the necessity of resorting to the throne of grace, that he may obtain mercy, and find grace to help in time of need.

2. SELFISHNESS is the other great centre of human depravity. It is not necessary to prove that selfishness in its highest degree reigns in every human heart, for undoubtedly there are some on whom this taint has fallen much less heavily than the taint of godlessness. Yet the

very fact that selfishness in the vilest forms swarms on every side, even in the bosom of a community professedly Christian, may surely convince us that the deadly virus has got an alarming hold on the whole family of man. A large class among us musters undisguisedly under the motto, 'Every man for himself;' and among the members of the fraternity there is no want of loyalty to their banner. See how eagerly many clutch at the highest gains they can procure, utterly regardless of the interests of others; how the trader will push his opium or his ardent spirits among communities which they are sure to enslave or debase; how the slave-dealer will depopulate the fairest regions of the globe, and not scruple to burn and pillage, to mutilate and murder on every side, in order to make up the gang which he has undertaken to provide; how the sensualist will lure his victim to his haunts, in spite of the broken hearts of parents, and the infallible ruin that awaits herself; how the whole business of parliaments, and courts of justice, and police institutions is mainly to create checks and safeguards against human selfishness, and to secure that if men will not live in brotherly love they shall at least pay some regard to the rights of neighbours and brethren weaker than themselves. Can it be that a mortal disease, which on the very face of society is seen to be so widely spread, has passed over any member of the family without leaving behind even one trace of its presence?

But let us not think of selfishness merely in its vilest forms. Our Lord himself has furnished us with a test which enables us to detect it in forms as subtle as any in which the chemist detects the presence of poison. It is the golden rule, 'Whatsoever ye would that men should do to you, do ye also unto them;' or, what is in substance the same, 'Thou shalt love thy neighbour as thyself.' Whoever fails to do this is selfish. To the extent to which he fails, he is selfish. What character, however amiable, could stand the test? Where is the man who has always been as concerned for his neighbour's comfort as for his own; who has always paid as much regard to his neighbour's feelings as his own; who has never sought to benefit himself or exalt himself at the expense of others; who has never grudged trouble in doing that for another which he would have done for himself; who even in his inmost heart has never felt a touch of envy when another was prospering beyond him, or a thrill of satisfaction when one who had been an enemy and opponent began to feel the grip of adversity! The truth is that the more unselfish men are, the more sensitive are their consciences, and the more ready are they to condemn themselves for breaches of the law of charity unperceived and unsuspected by coarser and rougher minds. Looking to so much higher a standard than the mass of men, they are the more ready to feel and confess their shortcomings; and the very compliments that often flow on them so copiously from their fellows, by recalling the host of heart-sins which no eye perceives but their own, only lead to a deeper humiliation and a more absolute sense of unworthiness in the sight of God.

Yes, there is a seed of selfishness, more or less developed, in all men. But undoubtedly it is the godlessness of the natural heart that furnishes the main article of the indictment in which all men are declared guilty before God. The root of the evil is, the secret aversion of man to the Living God, his inward recoil from the Holy One, and the deadness of his heart in respect of those emotions that ought to flow out from it to God in clouds of fragrance. Dead to God! Who can fathom the depths of the unworthiness which that state of things implies? A heart dead to a loving parent, dead to a generous friend, dead to a devoted spouse, stands at a fearfully low point in the scale of depravity; but what can be thought of a heart dead to GOD! And as the guilt is great, so is the resulting evil. More than the creeping plant depends on the stake or trellis, more than the feeble infant depends on its mother—man is formed to depend on God. God is the fountain of his being, the only source in him of order, beauty, life, and progress. Without God everything falls into confusion. Noisome lusts come creeping as from their dens, and leave their slime on the fairest features of the soul. The reins are torn by appetite and passion from the hands of conscience and reason; the texture of the soul is unknit; and there is no force in it to subdue the rebellion. Souls that have been restored through God's grace in Christ have no stronger conviction than that all their springs are in God, and that if the blessed connection that has been formed between them were for one moment to be severed, that moment they would wither and rot like a fallen leaf. It is this sense of dependence, absolute, constant, and entire, that gives such pathos to some of our hymns, expressive of the breathings of the earnest heart :—

> 'Other refuge have I none,
>   Hangs my helpless soul on Thee;
> Leave, ah, leave me not alone,
>   Still support and comfort me.

> All my trust in Thee is stayed,
> All my help from Thee I bring;
> Cover my defenceless head
> With the shadow of Thy wing.'

Who of us have got this blessed fellowship? Have you awoke from the dark dream of your self-confident heart that you could do well enough without God? Have you come to see that God is indispensable to your very being? Have you been made to shiver in looking back on the past, at the thought of a life spent without God; and still more in looking forward to the future, at the prospect of an endless existence divorced from His presence and darkened by His frown? Have you fled for refuge to take hold of the hope set before you? and have you found at the cross of Jesus the blessedness of Divine acceptance and fellowship, and learned to know the joy, and to sing the hymn, of the reconciled and comforted—'O Lord, I will praise thee; though thou wast angry with me, thine anger is turned away, and thou comfortedst me.'

II.

GOD'S SENTENCE ON MAN.

IT is a miserable interval that elapses, in a great and exciting trial, between the verdict of the jury and the sentence of the judge. Miserable to the spectators, miserable to the judge, and supremely miserable to the criminal. The last ray of hope is extinguished in the prisoner's horizon. The blackness of darkness seems to reign. There is nothing for him but to bow the soul in blank despair to the stroke which is to crush it in the dust, apparently for ever.

It shows the sad apathy of men in spiritual things, that while human verdicts and human sentences are received with such emotion, men are naturally so little concerned either as to the Divine verdict on their conduct, or the Divine sentence on their guilt.* No doubt, as things usually go on in the world, we want the excitement and concentrated attention of a trial. There is nothing to rivet the eye or overpower the senses, or to constrain men to feel that their eternal destinies are trembling in the balance. The forbearance of the judge often hardens the heart, and 'because sentence against an evil work is not executed speedily, the hearts of the children of men are fully set in them to do evil.' But is it not strange that men can read in the Word of God, that they are all guilty in his sight, and receive the tidings with so little emotion? Nay, more, that they can take the announcement very much as a matter of course, the consequences of which need in no way trouble them? And that instead of earnestly inquiring, what is the sentence attached by their judge to the guilt which has been proved against them, and whether there is a possibility of that sentence being repealed, they eat and drink, and joke and play, in utter regardlessness, as men did the day when Noah entered the ark, and as they shall still be doing when the sign of the Son of man appears in heaven?

We have seen God's verdict on man—all the world become GUILTY before God. We have examined some of the grounds of the verdict, and have found that no human being can escape the charge of ungodliness and selfishness. It is plain that no man born of woman is just before God. We are all transgressors of a law that is holy and just and good. What is the consequence? Is our transgression simply a thing to be regretted, regretted in heaven and regretted on earth, but merely regretted? Is it to be regarded simply as an untoward event, lessening our happiness, and hindering our progress, no doubt, but not leading to more serious evil? Is it like a break-down in a journey, or an accident at sea, a distressing occurrence in itself, but of which we must just try to make the best, and go crippling on, as best we may? Such is undoubtedly the feeling and the philosophy of many in our day. Human nature, unfortunately, has got crippled somehow. The machinery has got out of gear, and is not working very comfortably or very efficiently. Well, it is no doubt a pity. But just let us be patient. Let us try to make the best of it. Let us calmly examine what is wrong, and endeavour to adjust it, as you would disentangle a hank of ravelled worsted. All will come right by-and-by. But don't let us be frightened by the thought of punishment, or anything of that kind. Don't let us get disheartened with depressing views of our unworthiness. God is merciful and full of compassion. Surely we may expect He will be ready to help us in repairing this catastrophe, and not fall on us, like an angry tyrant, terrifying us with vengeance, and driving us to despair.

This is an easy view of the situation, and recommends itself to many a mind. But even before we go to the Word of God to compare it with its testimony, let us see whether there be not a voice in our bosoms that utters a different sound. Are there no remains in us of a conscience that testifies that when wrong has been done, punishment is due? If I rob, or steal, or lie, or cheat, am I able to comfort myself with the thought that it is a mere derangement of my moral machinery, and that it would be both foolish and wrong to dream of punishment? Or if my self-love flatters me that in my own case this is the right view of the matter, is my judgment the same when the guilty party is another? When Nathan comes to me with a story of shameful wrong,—of a rich man that, when a stranger came to him, forbore to take of his own flocks wherewith to entertain him, but seized the poor man's ewe lamb that had grown up together with him and his children, that did eat of his own meat, and drank of his own cup, and lay in his bosom, and was unto him as a daughter,—is there no indignant voice that sounds out from my breast, 'The man that hath done this thing shall surely die?' And if the prophetic story has been but a disguise, designed to secure my verdict before I recognize the criminal, how absolutely condemned and silenced I must lie when he looks me in the face, and says to me, 'Thou art the man!'

'If our own hearts condemn us, God is greater than our hearts, and knoweth all things.' When we open our Bibles, and inquire what is taught there as to the sentence and fruit of sin, we find nothing to allay the terrors of conscience, but the case much worse than we had even supposed.

1. In the first place, we find passages almost without number that declare death to be the punishment of sin. 'In the day thou eatest thereof, thou shalt surely die.' 'The soul that sinneth, it shall die.' 'The wages of sin is death.' 'By one man sin entered into the world, and death by sin.' If we ask what this death means, we find abundant evidence that it is a condition of most grievous pain and suffering. 'The smoke of their torment ascendeth up for ever and ever.' It is, moreover, a state of abandonment,—of

separation from all gracious, blessed influences,—banishment from the Lord, consignment to the place where He hath forgotten to be gracious. Hence it is also a state of moral dissolution and spiritual death; unholy feelings have the mastery of the soul; unable to recover itself, unable to restore the dominion of love and purity, it is like the troubled sea when it cannot rest, whose waters cast up mire and dirt. Its element is the outer darkness, where there is weeping, and wailing, and gnashing of teeth.

2. There is no part of the Bible where this is more frequently taught, or rather assumed as the doom of sin, than that which contains our Lord's own discourses—the four Gospels. Underneath the whole course of our Lord's teaching, there lay the awful truth that man is lost and ruined, and that it needs but a touch, as it were, to precipitate the catastrophe, and plunge him into the abyss. The herald of Christ's kingdom made men familiar with 'the wrath to come,' and announced the coming of One who would 'gather

the wheat into his garner, and burn up the chaff with unquenchable fire.' And though the sermon on the mount begins with a garland of blessings, it makes it plain that these are only for the redeemed children of the kingdom, and that mankind at large are separated by but a thin crust, as it were, from horrible ruin. How often, in that sermon, does Jesus withdraw the veil, and give us a glimpse of the world of woe! As when He warns us that it is better for us that one of our members should perish, than that our whole body should be cast into hell. As when He cautions us against the spirit of anger, and startles us by saying that to call a brother 'Thou fool,' is to make ourselves in danger of hell-fire. As when He points to the doom of the hypocrites 'in that day,' for whom no place can be found in the kingdom of heaven, and whose sentence is, 'Depart from me, ye that work iniquity.' The very sermon that opens with words of blessing closes with the sound of destruction,—the ruin of the house built on the sand; as if the Lord could not dismiss the feeling that, spite of all He came to offer to men, and spite of all His earnestness in offering it, destruction was the doom to which multitudes of them would finally come.

The same thing is true of all Christ's ministry. He speaks and teaches all through like one solemnized and saddened by the awful fact of man's ruin through sin. He is moved with compassion as He sees the multitude walking on the broad road and going to destruction,—all but the few who have been persuaded to enter in at the strait gate. Now He warns us not to fear them that kill the body, but rather to fear Him who can destroy both soul and body in hell. Now He tells us of the rich man that lifted up his eyes in hell being in torment. Now of the foolish virgins that had no oil in their lamps, and found the door shut when they would have joined the bridegroom. Now of the guest that came to the feast without the wedding garment, and was cast into outer darkness, amid weeping and gnashing of teeth. Now of the dread assize, when the

Son of man appears in His glory, and sets the sheep on His right hand and the goats on His left. Now He warns Capernaum, that exalted though she had been to heaven, she would be brought down to hell. Anon Chorazin and Bethsaida are reproached with their unbelief, and told that it would be more tolerable for Sodom and Gomorrah than for them in the day of judgment. And when He speaks of His clients it is as of persons condemned and ruined. 'The Son of man is come to seek and to save that which is lost.' 'God so loved the world that he gave his only begotten Son, that whosoever believeth on him *should not perish,* but should have everlasting life.' The rescue of a single sinner is such a glorious event that there is joy over him in the presence of the angels of God; and the best and truest representation both of the nature of the deliverance and the joy which it awakens, is found in the exclamation of the father of the prodigal: 'This my son was *dead,* and is alive again; he was *lost,* and is found.'

It is amazing that this great element of Christ's teaching should have failed to arrest universal attention, and that in some of those able books on the life of Christ that have lately appeared, no notice should have been taken of it, in the enumeration of the great lessons of his ministry. The fact is, and it is a most instructive and remarkable one, that in Christ's own discourses there are more references to hell and its punishments than in all other parts of the Bible put together. Though He came to reveal the Father, and pre-eminently to reveal His love; though the angels sung at His birth, 'Glory to God in the highest, on earth peace, good-will to men;' though every utterance of His lips was steeped in love, and all His garments smelled of myrrh and aloes and cassia out of the ivory palaces, He nevertheless spoke more, and more frequently, of hell, than any other inspired teacher whatever. The only one of the Apostles that in any marked degree followed up this line of teaching was that beloved disciple whose heart bore the closest resemblance to Christ's own; but in his case it was rather symbolical pictures of retribution than direct lessons on hell that he was commissioned to communicate. And is there not something very solemn and very touching in the fact that to so large a degree our blessed Lord reserved this awful line of instruction to Himself? On the one hand, does it not show how deeply He was impressed with the reality of hell,—how some plaintive dirge like that of the 'Dies Iræ' seemed ever to sound in His ears,—how the awful fact that sin had made hell the eternal prison of lost humanity haunted His tender soul, and gave untold bitterness to His tears, depth to His pity, and tenderness to His pleadings? Does it not go far, too, to account for the bursts of holy indignation which He poured out from time to time on the scribes and Pharisees, who seemed to be exerting all their energies to hinder the escape of the lost, and thrust them back into their horrid prison? On the other hand, does it not show us that, in the view of our blessed Lord, this whole subject of everlasting punishment was too solemn to be handled by common hearts or in common moods, and that a wrong impression of it was liable to be conveyed, unless it were set forth in the spirit of most gentle compassion and longing love? Who can estimate the evil done by those rough and hard-hearted denunciations of woe in which some indulge, and which even from Protestant pulpits are no better than Papal or Pagan anathemas? Or how can we sufficiently deplore the fact, that when men are most excited by passion and debased by sensuality, it is from this region they are most prone to fetch their epithets of abuse! that the mention of hell and damnation, which our blessed Lord so earnestly sought to associate with the deepest solemnity and the tenderest awe, should be connected, in the experience of multitudes, only with the most savage passions and brutalities of the vilest of mankind!

We must remember, at the same time, that while our Lord thus assumed and dealt with the lost condition of men, He never confounded their several shades of guilt, or their several degrees of punishment. He left abundant room for discrimination between the servant that knew his Lord's will and the servant that knew it not; and while He made it quite plain that, in the case of those to whom He was appealing, and all in similar circumstances, the great law of punishment would take the fullest effect if they disregarded His voice, He showed such reserve in alluding to the future doom of communities, like Tyre and Sidon, or Sodom and Gomorrah, as ought to repress all harsh speculation on our part as to their future condition, and make us fall back in patient trust on the soothing and assuring thought—'Shall not the Judge of all the earth do right?'

3. If we seek for still further evidence of God's sentence on sinful man, we shall find it in the experience of all in whom the Holy Spirit begins the new life by convincing them of sin. The starting-point of that life is the sense of ruin, the consciousness of being exposed to everlast-

ing misery—sometimes springing up in the soul with instantaneous suddenness, and sometimes beginning quietly, and gradually increasing in strength, until at last it becomes insupportable.

Thus, on the great day of Pentecost, the first evidence of a Divine work was seen when the thousands were pricked in their heart, and said to Peter and the rest of the Apostles, 'Men and brethren, what shall we do?' They felt themselves condemned and lost; God's verdict and sentence of death against them as sinners, were borne home to their consciences by the power of the Holy Spirit; and that great instinct of self-preservation which makes us shrink from approaching hurt and destruction was roused into unprecedented activity, because their danger seemed to come from the Author of their being, and the destruction that hung over them was infinite and everlasting.

The intensity of men's convictions may differ greatly according to the measure and manner of the power exerted by the Spirit, and the temperament and circumstances of the persons themselves. But unless there has been produced in men's hearts, at some time and in some way, a real sense of sin and condemnation, leading to a real acceptance of the Saviour and His work, there can be no reliance on the permanence of their impressions; their goodness may be but as the morning cloud and the early dew.

Christianity answers to all the wants of man's nature, the more superficial as well as the more profound. It answers, for example, to his desire of knowledge, his admiration of what is noble and disinterested, his craving for sympathy, his love of rest, his longing for a happier world, his ardent desire for re-union with all whom he has loved and lost. Taking hold of such feelings as these, Christianity exerts a measure of influence on many. But if no deeper cravings have been stirred, and no firmer grip has been taken, of the soul, its serious feelings may change with the seasons, and even vanish like a dream. Doubtless it was such superficial impressions that our

Lord meant to indicate in this parable of the sower, by the seed on stony ground that sprung up so rapidly, but as soon as the sun was up, withered away, because it had no root and no deepness of earth. To endure for ever, and bring forth fruit, religion must take hold on the deepest wants of our nature. It must come to us as lost sinners, in fact, bringing us the salvation that we need. It must come to us as the rope comes to the shipwrecked sailor, as food comes to the famished traveller, as a reprieve comes to the condemned malefactor. We must take hold on Christ, not merely because He is a nobler character than Brahma or Mahomet; not merely because His religion has a gentler spirit and a purer aim; not merely because the New Jerusalem is a fairer city, and its music of a sweeter strain; not merely because the scriptural vision of Paradise Regained is the brightest we have ever known or fancied;—but, emphatically, because we are condemned criminals, and Christ only can pardon us; because our hearts are under sin, and Christ only can free us; because we are unfit for holy fellowship, and Christ only can make us meet to be partakers of the inheritance of the saints in light; in a word, because we are wretched, and miserable, and poor, and naked, and blind; and no store but that of Christ's fulness can provide the blessings out of which such numberless wants can be supplied.

When any one's heart is truly under the convincing power of the Holy Ghost, there are at least two views of his state that give rise to the conviction that he is justly condemned in the sight of God.

In the first place, many are overwhelmed by a sense of the guilt of their past lives. It is *the past* that appals them. All along, from very infancy to the moment when conscience awoke, they see nothing but a career of guilt. The grand purpose of their lives neglected; the great God, whose their breath is, treated with indifference, His holy law trampled under foot, self-indulged and humoured in a thousand forms, irregular lusts and passions tolerated;—all these, varied perhaps by deeper and darker crimes, seem strewn in dismal profusion along their bygone lives. It is not as if they had been labouring in the main to serve God, and here and there had failed. It seems rather as if God had been utterly neglected, had not received from them one act of genuine service, one throb of filial affection, or one feeling of loyal devotion. A glimpse of the bright devotion and service of the angels gives a deeper shade to the guilt that shrouds their life. And when they come to see God in His true character, as revealed in Christ, rich in mercy and overflowing with love, yet infinitely holy, the sense of their unworthy conduct becomes overwhelming. 'God be merciful to me a sinner,' is the prayer that rushes to their lips; 'if thou, Lord, shouldest mark iniquity, O Lord, who shall stand?'

There are others, again, who are overwhelmed chiefly by the sense of their present or current deficiencies in the sight of God. It is the present, rather than the past, that appals them. Let them try their very best, they cannot come near to the requirements of God's holy law. Iniquities are ever prevailing against them. The heart is like a mint, coining ungodly feelings in guilty profusion. Though you were to assure them of pardon for the past, it would matter but little, so long as their ungodly hearts were there to pour out fresh streams of corruption and wickedness. They mourn most bitterly their diseased, sin-ridden nature. How is that polluted fountain ever to be turned into a crystal stream? Each time they survey their hearts they see fresh evidence of the awful virulence of the leprosy that has assailed them, and feel disposed, like the leper of old, to rend their clothes and bare their heads, and exclaim, 'Unclean! unclean!' In spite of their most earnest efforts, despair would seize them, were there no free grace to brighten their prospects. The forlorn and exhausted traveller who has lost his way in a wintry night, and after shouting himself hoarse, and dragging his limbs through drifting snow, till he can drag no longer, feels as if there were nothing for him but to lie down and sleep the sleep that knows no waking, does not experience half such joy and relief, when a light hard by suddenly reveals a friendly cottage, as the sinner, wearied in his vain efforts to purify his heart, feels when he hears the voice of Jesus—'Come unto me, all ye that labour and are heavy laden, and I will give you rest.'

No doubt it seems a hard doctrine that in the sight of God all men are under condemnation. Human nature sometimes appears in so interesting a light that it seems as if none but the most heartless of men could believe that all lie under the sentence of death. Gentle beings come on the scene, whose very looks of love and goodness seem to warm the air and 'make a sunshine in the shady place;' noble-hearted men spring forward to deeds of generosity and self-denial that draw one long burst of applause from every spectator; and it seems horrible to suppose that such persons are to be regarded as 'children of wrath, even as others.' The doctrine of the Bible is that they are so *by nature*. Who can tell but that very gentleness and generosity are fruits of grace? It is certain that 'every good and perfect gift is from above, and cometh down from the Father of lights, with whom there is no variableness, or shadow of turning.' Happily, we are not required to judge what degree of consciousness of renewal there must be during the introduction of the divine life into any heart, and its establishment there with a preponderating power. This is one of the deep things of God, from which, in many instances, He has not been pleased to remove the veil of mystery. Men are only too ready to tear away the veil left by God, and to constitute themselves judges of the spiritual state of their brethren. But let us grant that beautiful features may appear in the character of the unregenerate, in the character of men whom the will of God does not habitually sway, and who have no knowledge of the grace of God in Christ. It does not follow that because of these beautiful features they are not under the condemnation of God. A chain may have some admirable links in it, and yet be as unserviceable as a hempen cord. An old abbey may present a perfect arch or a beautiful capital here and there, and yet be an utter ruin. A ship may show a beautifully carved prow, or a faultless deck, and yet be as unfit for sea as the coarsest raft that was ever nailed together. The question is not whether men or women have some interesting and attractive features about them. You generally find that in the character even of the bacchanalian there is a sort of jovial good-humour, which is attractive to his companions, and contributes to the hilarity of the social hour. But this flowing joviality may exist side by side with the spirit that breaks the heart of a gentle wife, and leaves the offspring of his own body unclothed, unfed, untaught, uncared for. So also there may be bursts of generosity and gleams of gentleness in natures that show great deficiency under the strain of ordinary duty. Account for such beautiful features as we may, they in no way clash with the truth that men by nature lie under a sentence of death in the sight of God. Who that is weighed in the balances of the All-holy One shall not be found wanting? Who shall escape the condemnation due to those that have failed in the great end of life—have worshipped and served the creature more than the Creator, who is blessed for evermore? Who can affirm that, without any renewing process from above, the power of good in his nature preponderates above the power of evil, and that he finds within himself strength sufficient to conquer in every conflict, the lust of the flesh, the lust of the eye, and the pride of life —all, in short, that is not of the Father, but of the world? No doubt there may be found men who affirm that they do all this, just as the young man in the Gospel most honestly assured Christ that he had kept all the commandments from his youth. But as our blessed Lord had in reserve a test of fidelity to high duty which even this young man could not stand, so must all boasters and self-complacent flatterers find, in the great day of judgment, that their standard has been miserably defective, and their performance infinitely inadequate. While the weather continues calm and mild, it is easy to live in a house built upon the sand. It is when the rain descends, and the wind comes, and beats upon that house, that its real feebleness is discovered, and its helpless inhabitant buried in the ruins. Sometimes, even in this life, the self-satisfied pharisee is disturbed in his fancied security. The sick bed brings him nearer to God, and in that clearer and holier light, his life has an ugly look, and he trembles to look forward. If the few streaks, as it were, of divine light that penetrate by the sick chamber into the soul, can shake his confidence, what must he feel in the full blaze of the judgment-seat? For 'the loftiness of man shall be bowed down, and the haughtiness of men shall be brought low: and the Lord alone shall be exalted in that day.'

It is vain to make out that we are clean in the sight of God. Strive as he may, the Ethiopian cannot change his skin, nor the leopard his spots. Infinitely better at once to give up the conflict; to let the divine light in freely upon our hearts and lives; to admit the justice of the divine sentence against us; to cease to dispute the truth that 'the wages of sin is death;' and to find our comfort in the glorious counter-truth, 'the gift of God is eternal life through Jesus Christ our Lord.'

III.

THE EVIL OF SIN.

WHEN the ostrich, scouring along the sandy desert, finds that it cannot escape the huntsman, it is said to thrust its head into a bush, and remain there, quite tranquil, to receive the death-blow. Poor senseless, stupid bird, it seems to fancy that the danger which it ceases to see has ceased to exist. But men, as well as brutes, do so; and not by one degree more rational than the composure of a bird at whose folly they themselves would be the first to smile, is the peace of those who, that they may enjoy the pleasures of sin, shut their eyes to its evil, and refuse to look that, and their own danger, in the face. I do not deny that they, having persuaded themselves that sin is a trivial thing, and by no means, to use the language of Scripture, 'exceeding sinful,' enjoy a sort of peace. They have laid the flattering unction to their souls that God is all merciful—that they have not been great sinners—that they have done no one harm, but themselves perhaps—that many people are worse than they—and that however they may have sinned, the prayers and penitence of a death-bed shall set all right. But I have seen the administration of an opiate produce a similar effect—casting a man into so deep a slumber that he felt no pain. But for the low whispers of the attendants, the solemn stillness of the room, and the anxious countenances of those that were watching by his side, none would have fancied that a mortal disease was raging within his vitals, and hurrying him on to the grave. And not more different this sleep from tired nature's healthful slumbers, than the peace of the ungodly from his who is resting by faith on Jesus, and has made his 'calling and election sure.'

Nor is it only exemption from 'the stings' of conscience a man may enjoy who shuts his eyes to the evil of sin. He may enjoy positive happiness of a kind; and be to appearance blither and in better spirits than better men. What of that? So is yon drunkard, who has drowned all his sorrows with his senses in the flowing bowl—the ragged wretch who, untouched by the sad looks of the broken-hearted wife and children that sit cowering, shivering over some miserable embers, stands on the floor of his dismantled home, and casts idiot smiles on the wreck around him. I do not deny that there is pleasure in sin. Were it not so, there would be fewer sinners. But when I look at its end—that 'the way of transgressors is hard'—how justly may it be compared to the delirium of sailors who, when the bonds of order are broken, and all further efforts to save themselves and their ship are abandoned, hoist the spirit cask on deck, and maddening their brains with drink, go down into the deep amid shouts of laughter and songs of merriment.

Even so, many, intoxicated with the pleasures of sin, go down into perdition.

There is a state worse, more hopeless perhaps, than either of these. They stand in great danger of damnation who shut their eyes to the evil of sin, but they in greater who, practising iniquity till conscience grows seared and dead, have ceased to feel its evil. Such in some cases is their apathy that it seems as if God had cast them off, and said, provoked by their long-continued resistance to the remonstrances of conscience and of his word and Spirit, 'He is joined to his idols, let him alone.' There lies our danger if we are trusting for salvation to a death-bed repentance. People think they will be very much alarmed at the approach of death. There is no greater mistake: the greatest wonder death-beds show, and ministers see, being not the calmness with which a believer dies, but the insensibility, the deep, unmoved, and unmoveable apathy with which others meet death. 'There are no bands in their death—they are not in trouble as other men,' as the Bible says. By their dying-bed—no place for flattery, or 'healing the hurt of the daughter of God's people slightly'—they have been told the most alarming truths; I have thundered the law of Sinai in their ears; I have set forth a dying Saviour with the love of Calvary before their eyes, but it produced neither a response nor emotion. Fearing nothing, if hoping nothing, they have gone to their 'own place' more calmly than many a saint who dies in Jesus' arms, and leaves earth for heaven.

It is said of the rich man in the parable that 'in hell he lift up his eyes, being in torment.' Alas, it is too late—too late then to get our eyes opened; and therefore I shall try, with prayer for God's blessing, to set before my readers some considerations calculated to demonstrate and illustrate the *evil of sin*.

There is a cruel deception often practised on the dying. They are left to indulge hopes of life after their case is hopeless; the friends who were parties to this deception—if friends they can be called—thereby laying up for themselves a source of unavailing regrets. If people are true Christians, it is of no moment, or at least of little moment, that they should know themselves to be dying: but if otherwise, the sooner they know the worst the better; for who can tell but God may call at the eleventh hour? There is something more culpable and cruel than concealment of the truth. The dying are not left to deceive themselves, but are deceived. Every, the most remote, allusion to death is positively forbidden: ingenuity is taxed by schemes of future pleasure, books of light reading, and amusements to divert the mind from solemn thoughts, and keep them 'cheerful,' as it is called: as new and more fatal symptoms arise, they are carefully concealed: they may be shed without the dying chamber, but no tears are allowed, nor sorrow on any face within it; and so the play, the pitiful tragedy, goes on till the poor victim of mistaken kindness is hurried away into an unexpected, and perhaps unprepared for, eternity. Verily, 'the tender mercies of the wicked are cruel.'

But that expression applies with still more force to those who, called to be ambassadors of Jesus Christ, shrink from setting forth the inherent evil and awful punishment of sin—that, in the words of Scripture, 'it is an evil and a bitter thing to sin against the Lord!' Some will not tolerate any allusion to hell, beyond the most distant—and that with bated breath. They cannot abide to hear of it; denouncing him as a gloomy preacher who, not for his own pleasure but others' profit, ventures on this awful and most sad subject to declare the whole counsel of God. They say, 'Prophesy unto us smooth things.' The storm rages, the ship is sinking; yet they deem him an intruder on their peace who attempts to wake them, crying, 'What meanest thou, O sleeper? arise and call upon thy God!' There are certainly more agreeable topics—the goodness of God, which should lead us to repentance—the love of Christ, which should sweetly constrain us to live to Him who died for us—the joys of heaven, which by virtue of their superior attractions should withdraw our affections from the things that are seen and temporal to those that are unseen and eternal. No doubt also it is not so much by driving as by drawing that sinners are ordinarily brought to Jesus: and it is a far more agreeable task to melt a hard heart by arguments of kindness, than attempt to break it by arguments of fear—to work with the fire than with the hammer, God's word being compared to both. Yet the same apostle who, scattering Christ's blessed name as thick on his epistles as God has done stars in the nightly firmament, sought to constrain men by the love of Christ, persuades them also by the terrors of the Lord. He who asked, 'Despisest thou the riches of his goodness, and forbearance, and long-suffering, not knowing that the goodness of God leadeth to repentance?' also asked, 'Thinkest thou, O man, that thou shalt escape the judgment of God?' 'Knowing the terror of the Lord,' said St Paul, 'we persuade men.' Hence his tears, and these touching words, 'I have told you often, and now tell you even weeping, that they are the enemies of the cross of Christ, whose end is destruction.' No wonder he wept. The wonder is that we can read with so little emotion what fell in trembling accents from the Saviour's lips—of a worm that never dieth, and a fire that is never quenched. Why are we so callous? Why is not our pity so moved, and our hearts melted, and our fears awakened for poor careless sinners, that we might adopt the language of the Psalmist, and say, 'Rivers of waters run down mine eyes, because they keep not thy law!'

The way of transgressors is indeed hard; and we see the nature of sin plainly revealed in its dreadful effects. For there are two methods by which we may arrive at a knowledge of the nature of anything; we may either analyze its properties, or discover them by studying its effects. Taking, for instance, a deadly drug—I may, on the one hand, by analysis, find it to be composed of elements highly deleterious and fatal to life; on the other hand, I may take the shorter and more impressive method of administering it to some of the inferior creatures, and see the virulence of the poison in the violence of its effects—horrible convulsions and a speedy death. Some poisons are so deadly that a grain or a few drops of them is as fatal as a ball through the brain, or a knife stuck into the heart. To such a poison sin may with truth be compared; and nothing but their ignorance or disregard of its deadly nature would allow men to tamper with it, or speak lightly of the smallest sin.

It may be difficult for analysis to convey to some any sense of the evil that lies in all sin; but, surely, that may be understood by contemplating its effects. A child could understand the force latent in a cup of water, on seeing it, when converted into steam, rend asunder a plate of iron, or a mass of solid rock; or the power of lightning, if he saw it in the thunderstorm leap dazzling from the clouds, and striking some stately tree rive its trunk, and scatter its leafy glories on the ground; or the venom of the cobra's fang, on seeing the reptile raise its hooded crest to strike, and him it struck reel, and fall, and die at his feet. Let sin, in like manner, be tried by its effects; and who, with a mind enlightened, can look on the sad change it has wrought on man, on the divine beauty it defaced, on the favour it forfeited, on the happiness it wrecked, on the curse it has entailed and the fire it has kindled, on the misery it breeds in time and perpetuates in eternity, without seeing 'sin become exceeding sinful.' Look at Eden! Man's disobedience there, his plucking the forbidden fruit, may seem to some a trivial offence; but does the misery it brought on Adam, and entailed on his posterity throughout all generations, justify such a term? Put a case.

Suppose some day, when passing the house of one revered for his piety, and universally respected for his character, and known to be the gentlest and kindest and most affectionate of fathers, you saw him driving from his door the son and daughter he had loved, and cherished, and lived with in sweetest fellowship—with sad but stern voice ordering them out of his presence, you would stand amazed; but you would neither need him, nor any one else, to assure you that before he had driven forth these weeping ones to want, and shame, and sorrow, they had been guilty of some most aggravated crime—an offence no father could pass by, or palliate, or lightly pardon. But the love God bore to His human children has far transcended any that beats or burns in a father's or mother's bosom, as the heavens rise above the earth; and who can see Him drive them from His presence, order them away, without feeling that there must be a guilt in sin which we have no line to fathom nor powers to comprehend! There had been no place of woe otherwise, for God has no pleasure in the death of him that dieth, nor is He willing that any should perish; nor otherwise had His beloved Son, betrayed by a friend, disowned by the creatures of His hand, and deserted by His Father and God, bled on the accursed tree. If sin was not exceeding sinful and hateful, a less noble victim had satisfied the demands of justice, and a less dreadful expiation upheld the honour of a broken law. How deep the stain which it required the blood of God's own Son to wash out! How heavy the burden beneath which He sank, whose arms sustain the universe! What sorrows those which forced from His patient lips this cry, 'My soul is exceeding sorrowful, even unto death!'—the still more mysterious complaint of Calvary, ' My God, my God, why hast thou forsaken me?' If the virulence of a disease may be measured by the violence of its remedy, or the greatness of a debt by the sum paid for the discharge of the debtor, the evil that is in sin is as immeasurable as the love for which, with all his glowing piety and power of language, St Paul found no fitter expression than this, 'Oh the height and depth and breadth and length of the love of God, it passeth knowledge!'

A bitter thing, whether we contemplate its consequences here or hereafter, in this world or the next, sin undoubtedly is. It is more. That may be called bitter which, in a moral sense, is not evil—inherently and necessarily evil. Extreme poverty is bitter, as where a parent looks round on hungry and hollow-eyed children when there is neither fire on the hearth nor a morsel of food in the house—'When they cry for bread, and their mother has none to give them.' Yet there is no moral evil in poverty; it is no crime; on the contrary, 'hath not God chosen the poor of this world rich in faith and heirs of the kingdom?' It is a bitter thing, also, to lie under the hand of acute disease, tossing on a bed of pain, vainly turning from side to side for relief, counting the long night's lazy hours; when it is night, wearying for the morning; and when the morning comes, wearying for the night. Yet, in a moral sense, there is no evil here; on the contrary, while the outward man perisheth—strength turns to weakness, beauty to ghastly pallor, and symmetry to deformity—the inward man may be renewing day by day. It was a bitter thing for martyrs to suffer for righteousness' sake; to pine away in lonely exile; to perish on a scaffold; to be bound and burned at a stake. Yet, in a moral sense, it was not evil; on the contrary, Christ pronounced them 'blessed' who suffer; winning a martyr's crown, great is their reward in heaven.

Let us beware of looking on sin as we might on disease, or poverty, or persecution—our only dread its bitter consequences. Take these away; let death come, but not as a grim messenger summoning men to God's awful presence; let the grave give up its dead, but not to judgment; let there be a place of happiness, but none of misery; and many would see nothing in sin to shock their feelings or deter them from committing it—from drinking up iniquity as the ox drinketh up the water. But what an imperfect view of sin is theirs—imperfect as his of the crimes of robbery or murder who, were there no society to point the finger of scorn at him, nor prison to hold, nor judge to try, nor gallows to hang him, would steal your property, nor scruple to take your life. I believe no man can measure the depths of evil that are in sin; but he certainly has no adequate idea of them who, though sin should cease to be punished, and universal salvation were proclaimed from the skies, so that there were henceforth no hell, nor judgment, but heaven for all and hell for none, would cease to regard it as an evil thing— 'this abominable thing that I hate,' saith the Lord.

All the guilt that lies in foul rebellion against the mildest and most merciful of earthly monarchs—in disobeying the kindest, and grieving the best of fathers—in ingratitude to a generous benefactor—in returning cursing for blessing, evil for good, and hatred for favours, in wounding a heart that loves us and the hand that was stretched out to pluck us from destruction— in refusing to please One who, though rich, for our sakes made Himself poor; took our debts on Him and paid them; took our burdens on Him and carried them; and bearing disgrace to crown us with honour, saved our lives at the expense of His own;—all that evil, multiplied a thousand and a thousand times, there is in sin. It is a horrible crime committed against a gracious God and a loving Saviour—to say nothing of the injuries our sins have inflicted on ourselves, and the irreparable wrongs they may have done to others. It is from such views that true repentance springs. Are they ours? Different from the remorse of yon haggard and hardened wretch, who, at the door of a prison or the foot of a gallows, when his sins have found him out, sees their evil only in their punishment; it is not where the lake burns to consume, but Jesus bleeds to save, sin is seen in its greatest evil, and felt by God's people to be their deepest grief. 'They shall look on him whom they have pierced, and mourn as one mourneth for an only son, and be in bitterness as one is in bitterness for a first-born.' The importance of correct views of the evil that lies in sin cannot be exaggerated. To inadequate ideas of that may be traced the very imperfect conceptions some entertain of the necessity and great work of the atonement—of Christ, as our substitute, bearing our griefs and carrying our sorrows, and so opening up a passage for the ocean of divine love to flow out in the blessings of redemption on this lost and guilty world.

'Let every man,' says the Apostle, 'prove his own work;' and here, I may now remark, we have an admirable test whereby to try the genuineness of our faith and repentance. If our only motive for abstaining from sin lies in the dread of punishment, our obedience, such as it is, springs not from the love of God, but of ourselves. It is entirely selfish; and having no regard to Him whatever, it is in fact but a continual breaking of the law, 'Thou shalt love the Lord thy God with all thy heart, and with all thy soul, and with all thy mind, and with all thy strength.' Our case is like that of a servant who has a kind master, but obeys, not because he loves his master, but only his wages,—of a son, who, but for the dread of the rod, would treat a father's wishes with insolent contempt, and openly defy his authority. How can God set any value on such obedience? He Himself has answered the question, 'A son honoureth his father, and a servant his master; if then I be a father, where is mine honour? and if I be a master, where is my fear? If ye offer the blind for sacrifice, is it not evil? and if ye offer the lame and sick, is it not evil? Offer it now unto thy governor; will he be pleased with thee, or accept thy person, saith the Lord of hosts?' The test, therefore, by which to try the genuineness of our faith and repentance lies in this question, Would we sin were no punishment to follow?—in other words, 'Shall we continue in sin that grace may abound?' So Paul puts the question; and how does he answer it? Filled with holy horror at the impious thought, and speaking for all who have undergone a saving change, he replies, 'God forbid!' Does his emphatic exclamation find an echo in our breasts? Does sin appear to us so exceeding sinful that we would not commit it though we had read our names in the book of life, and felt as sure of heaven as if already there? Then, notwithstanding all our transgressions and shortcomings, we may take the comfort of these blessed words, 'Ye are washed, ye are sanctified, ye are justified in the name of the Lord, and by the Spirit of our God.'

These views of sin are no doubt calculated to humble us in our own esteem. Humble us? Let the Spirit of our God open our eyes fully to its exceeding sinfulness, and, overwhelmed by a sense of guilt and shame, we shall exclaim with Job, ' I abhor myself, and repent in dust and ashes.' Some, indeed, vain of themselves and of their own doings, maintain a self-complacent spirit, nor stand abashed in the presence of Him before whose glory, as a man screens his eyes from the blaze of the sun, angels veil their faces. How different from a humble Christian's the attitude of yonder Pharisee! See how, like the bird that, strutting proudly on the lawn, unfurls its gaudy tail to display its beauties to the sun, he presents himself for the admiration of God and man. 'I fast,' he says, 'twice in the week, I give tithes of all that I possess. I thank thee that I am not as other men, or even as this publican.'

But it is no evidence that we are abhorred of God, that we have been brought to abhor ourselves; on the contrary, 'The sacrifices of God are a broken spirit; a broken and a contrite heart, O Lord, thou wilt not despise.' 'I,' said St Paul, 'am the chief of sinners;' 'I,' said David, 'was as a beast before thee;' 'I,' said Ezra, ' am ashamed, and blush to lift up my face to thee, O my God, for our iniquities are increased over our heads, and our trespass is gone up unto the heavens;' and so certainly does a man grow humbler as he grows holier, that it is with self-esteem as with the column of mercury in the tube of a barometer—the higher we ascend, it sinks the lower. What more striking illustration of this than heaven itself affords? There, purified from all conceit and pride, perfect both in humility and in holiness, the saints, as if unworthy to wear on their heads what Jesus won on his cross, cast their crowns at his feet. There, with eyes death has purged, in purest rays serene, they see God—the true mirror in which to see ourselves. For as the best way to estimate the feebleness of a taper is not to measure the small space its rays illuminate, but to hold it up against the sun, and see its flame grow dull to blackness in the blaze of his burning beams; or as the best way to correct an exaggerated impression of the magnitude of the pyramids were not to measure their dimensions, but to transport them, were it possible, to the foot of some lofty mountain, the snow-crowned monarch of the Alps or Andes; so the best way of measuring ourselves is to measure ourselves with God. Seeing our littleness in His greatness, our vile ingratitude in His boundless goodness, the impurity of our hearts and the sinfulness of our lives in His ineffable and unspotted holiness, it is easy to understand how the best have been the humblest men; and how one, so distinguished for piety and beneficence as Job, should have exclaimed, 'I have heard of thee by the hearing of the ear, but now mine eye seeth thee: wherefore I abhor myself, and repent in dust and ashes.'

If this attempt to set forth the evil of sin has awakened, or deepened, any sense of my reader's need of a Saviour, if it has made him think less of himself and more of Christ, it is well. Self-abasement before God—the pledge that the publican went down to his house justified—has characterized not Job and David, not prophets and apostles only, but the elect of God in every age of the church. Read the life of any eminent saint; and from the glowing panegyric of his biographer turn to the page which records the man's opinion of himself; and how low the estimate, how different the language! The two seem to describe distinct persons; yet, dissimilar as are the portraits, one man sat for both. What hard things he has written against himself, what confessions of guilt and sin he has left, at whose death men exclaimed,

'A prince and a great man has fallen this day in Israel'—by whose grave a weeping church has raised the cry, 'My father, my father! the chariots of Israel and the horsemen thereof.' For example, how did Knox, the man above all other men whose name, as the greatest and bravest of her sons, is dear to Scotland, regard himself, estimate the mighty work he had lived to do? The poorest, vilest, most useless, never lay lower at the foot of the cross—there, tempted to indulge in self-satisfaction, he passed the last night of his life in mortal conflict with the enemy of souls, conquering, though the battle lasted through all its weary hours, by the blood of the cross. And who, to quote but another case, has not heard of John Wesley—how much, not England only, but the whole world owes to him, to his poetry and his piety, to his love for Christ and love for souls, to his burning zeal and apostolic labours? With his praise in all the churches, and a fame spread wide as the world itself, what estimate did he form of himself? what hopes sustained him in a dying hour? 'I have been reflecting,' he said, 'on my past life; I have been wandering up and down between fifty and sixty years, endeavouring in my poor way to do a little good to my fellow-creatures; and what have I to trust to for salvation? I can see nothing which I have done or suffered that will bear looking at. I have no other plea than this—

> "I the chief of sinners am,
> But Jesus died for me."'

IV.

MAN'S INABILITY TO SAVE HIMSELF.

TO a young man who came, saying, 'Good Master, what shall I do to inherit eternal life?' our Lord replied, 'Go thy way, sell whatsoever thou hast, and give to the poor, and thou shalt have treasure in heaven; and come, take up the cross, and follow me.' A hard saying that! To an aged saint a very difficult duty,—how much more to a babe in Christ, to one but entering, if entering, on the Christian life! It is not raw recruits and beardless boys, but veterans, men inured to war, to the flash of bayonet and the roar of cannon, that generals send to the front—where bullets are flying, and men are falling thickest. What man would order a sailor boy, the first day he trode the deck, to climb the shrouds, and reef the topsail in a storm, when the ship, caught in a hurricane, was plunging and tearing through the sea? Yet so our Lord dealt with this youth—putting him to a trial which the most advanced Christian would find it hard to bear.

Let us fancy ourselves in his circumstances. What a surprise to be called, all of a sudden, to part with our whole property, to leave home with its many tender ties, the scene of happy memories, the grave of beloved parents, the society of kind friends, the respect of the world, and the reputation of wealth, to descend, at one step, from affluence and comfort, to follow one himself so poor that he had no place where to lay his head! We cannot fancy the shock and the recoil we ourselves should feel, and not wonder that our Lord laid a load so heavy on a back so young.

But the apparent harshness in this case, as in many others, ceases when we know all its circumstances. What looks cruel comes out then as the truest kindness. We should make the greatest mistakes if we pronounced judgment on a remedy in ignorance of the disease it was meant to cure. You enter, for example, the theatre of an hospital. A pale, weak, wasted sufferer, with terror and anxiety in his face, is borne in, and laid on a blood-stained table. His arms are pinioned; and into the quivering flesh of him who needs rest rather than pain the surgeon buries a knife; —deaf to his entreaties, unmoved by his groans. This seems cruel, but it is not so. We have only to see the morbid mass separated from a form it had long tortured with pain, and was hurrying to an untimely grave, to see that the knife was both in a kind and skilful hand—that there was need of the knife, and life in the knife. Even so, on turning to St Matthew's account of this case, our Lord's apparent harshness changes into true kindness; all which seemed stern and hard entirely vanishing. He, who came to Jesus seeking eternal life, had no sense of his own inability to save himself; but fancied that he had only to be told how, and he could do it. In his account of the transaction, Mark represents him saying, 'Good Master, what shall I do to inherit eternal life?'—a form of the question not very different from the jailor's, when, seizing a light, he burst into the dungeon, and cast himself at the apostles' feet, to cry, 'Sirs, what shall I do to be saved?' Had that been the young man's question, springing up in his heart as in the jailor's, from feeling himself lost,—a poor, lost, helpless sinner,—this, doubtless, had been Christ's gracious and quick reply, 'Believe in me, and thou shalt be saved.' But the question, as more fully given by the Evangelist Matthew, is not simply, 'What shall I do to inherit eternal life?' but—a very different one—'What *good thing* shall I do to inherit eternal life?' Eternal life was a prize which, with some directions from Christ, he deemed himself able to win. Nor any wonder; for such was his ignorance of the nature of sin, of his own guilt and weakness, and how, spiritual in its nature, the law of God is violated as well by desires as by deeds, by wishes as by works, that to the repetition of the commandments he replied, with the most perfect self-complacency; 'Master, all these things have I kept from my youth.'

What is to be done in this case? It resembles that of one who, drugged with opium, has sunk into a deadly stupor; and to whom a stimulant has been administered without any good effect. The light is flashed on his dull, dilated pupils, but in vain; his pulse beats weaker, his breathing comes thicker, his lethargy grows more and more profound. Another and stronger stimulant is required. Unless he is roused he dies. So with this young man. He must be awoke to a sense of his real condition. He perishes otherwise, in his ignorance and sins. His case requires the strongest, and his salvation will justify the most painful remedies. For never, till he sees that he cannot save himself, will he repair to Jesus, and fall at His feet, to cry, 'Lord, save me; I perish!'

It was for that blessed purpose our Lord bade this man lay down the world, and take up the cross; His object being to make the man feel his need of Divine assistance and a new heart; and that, for all his talk about another world, he was glued to this one. But this could only be accomplished by putting the man to a trial. When in a calm, sunny day the ship rises and falls on the billows, she seems as free as the waves she rides—nor till the wind rises and swells her drooping sails, and, making no progress, she plunges and pitches like a steed under spur and rein, do we discover that beneath the water, unseen, and till then unsuspected, an anchor, with its iron arms, grasps the sand, chaining her to the earth. So, also, it is, when, turning her eye to the sun, and inspired with some love of freedom, the eagle, spreading out her wings and springing from the perch, attempts to fly, but has hardly mounted ere she drops down again, that we discover the noble bird to be a miserable captive, and see the chain that binds her to the earth. And our blessed Lord bade this man break loose from the world, and mount to heaven, to teach him by his very failure that he could not; that he had no power to save himself; that salvation is not of blood, nor of the will of the flesh, nor of the will of man—but of God: that, in his own words to Nicodemus, 'Except a man be born of water and of the Spirit, he cannot enter the kingdom of God.' And that doctrine I now proceed to illustrate.

This doctrine, I may, by way of introduction, observe, is evident from this, that the saved are all debtors to the free choice and grace of God.

A man of taste, wishing to stock a garden, waits till the seed he sows has sprung, and the plants that spring from it have flowered; and then, rejecting the rest, he selects for his parterres the flowers of fairest hue and finest forms. To stock an orchard, he pursues a similar course; waiting till time has proved their character, he selects the best trees, leaving such as are barren, or produce only inferior fruit, to be burned as fuel —the only thing they are fit for. Now, if man saves, or is capable of saving, himself, it were reasonable to expect that in bestowing on men everlasting life, God would have pursued a similar course. But amid all the dark mysteries that invest this subject, it is plain that He did not. It is not on our merits, but on His mercy, the choice turns; else what does the Apostle mean who says, 'Not by works of righteousness that we have done, but according to his mercy he saved us, by the washing of regeneration and renewing of the Holy Ghost, which He shed on us abundantly through Jesus Christ?' Not waiting till time has developed their character, as time does that of flowers and trees, God chooses those who are to be heirs of grace before their character is or can be formed—before their baptism, even before their birth; nor only before their birth, but before that of time itself—ere there was a man to sin, or a world to sin in; ere sun shone, or any angel sung. 'Blessed,' said Paul, with adoring gratitude, 'be the God and Father of our Lord Jesus, who hath blessed us with all spiritual blessings in heavenly places in Christ, according as he hath chosen us in him *before the foundation of the world.*' Chosen us, be it observed, not because we are holy; but making our holiness to be, not the cause, but the consequence of His choice—not the root it springs from, but the fruit it bears; 'chosen us,' he adds, 'that we should be holy and without blame before him in love.'

This truth—humbling to our pride, but placing our hopes on an immovable foundation—receives very remarkable and distinct expression in the reason which God assigned to Paul for requiring him to remain in Corinth. Steeped in the grossest idolatry, proverbial above any other in the world for unbridled licentiousness, the Apostle, who had succeeded in converting but a handful of its inhabitants, was about to leave that city; thinking that there no more good was to be done. Fancy his astonishment when God, appearing to him in a vision, said, 'Be not afraid, Paul, but speak, and hold not thy peace, for I am with thee, and no man shall set on thee to hurt thee; for I have *much people* in this city'—serving now at heathen altars, slaves now of the grossest vices, nevertheless they are my people; and here you are to abide, from these vile dust-heaps to gather out my jewels, from these dark depths of sin to bring up my pearls—they know not me, but I know them—they have not chosen me, but I have chosen them; not for their merits, but out of my mercy chosen them before the foundation of Corinth, or of the world itself. If God's ways are equal, unless there was one rule for the sinners of Corinth and another for us, none, therefore, are chosen from regard to their merits, or saved through their own ability—salvation being all of grace, pure and undeserved, as was once admirably brought out by a humble, unlettered Christian. Strong in faith, though not expert in argument, she answered the cavils of some who tried to puzzle her, as he who said to the Pharisees, 'This I know, that I once was blind, but now I see,'—she replied, 'This I know, that I never should have chosen God, unless God had first chosen me!'

I remark that our inability to save ourselves is evident from these, among many other considerations :—

1. We cannot plead guiltless of sin. Guiltless? What man so ignorant as to refuse his assent to the words of John, 'If we should say that we have no sin, we deceive ourselves—we make God a liar, and the truth is not in us?' In yonder temple, from which the crowd is rushing, priests, scribes, Pharisees, old and young, hustling each other in their haste, and leaving but our Lord, who stoops writing on the sanded floor, and a woman He has saved, for time at least—let us hope, she going to sin no more, for eternity—who had remained behind? Why this hot haste from the house of God? No fire has caught its beams; nor are its walls of mighty stones, rocked by an earthquake, cracking to their fall. Nothing but this has happened—a guilty woman has been dragged before Christ for doom; and He has pronounced the doom, but in this unexpected form, 'Let him that is without sin cast the first stone

at her!' Him that is without sin?—no hand is mouldering, nor shall any moulder in the dust to meet that condition, and execute the fatal sentence. For however irreproachable we appear in the sight of men, and more than irreproachable, respected, esteemed, and praised we may be of men, where in pew or pulpit is he who could hold up his hands before God, and say, 'These hands are clean!' We have all sinned; and since spiritual as well as temporal death has passed on all men because all have sinned, we are as unable to save ourselves as a dead man to leave his coffin, and return with the mourners who have carried him to the grave.

2. Our utmost efforts fall short of a perfect service. Such God's law requires; but who has ever reached, or even approached it?—who has satisfied the law, as summed up in these grand and lofty words, 'Thou shalt love the Lord thy God with all thy heart, and with all thy soul, and with all thy mind; and thy neighbour as thyself?' Not St Paul. He says, 'When I would do good,

evil is present with me.—That which I would, I do not, and that which I would not, that I do.' And where Paul failed, who can hope to succeed? To him who, in the splendour of his gifts and graces, shone without an equal when he lived, nor has had any successor since he died, dare any of us say, Stand aside, Paul, I am holier than thou? But suppose we could, what of that? The robe that, blanched by dews and rain and sunshine, seems so white beside the mould some hoary sexton flings from an open grave, turns dull and dingy laid on a bank of snow; and who, though he may seem an angel in the company of reprobates, of the profligate and profane, could stand comparison, side by side, with God's Son or God's holy law? Whom would not the contrast humble? —from whose lips call forth the language both of confession and prayer?—our confession, Job's, 'If I wash myself in snow-water and make my hands never so clean, yet shalt thou plunge me in the ditch and mine own clothes shall abhor me'— that our confession, and this, the Psalmist's, our prayer, 'Enter not into judgment with thy servant, for in thy sight shall no man living be justified!'

3. As sinners we are without excuse. Ere the judge condemns a man found guilty of a capital offence, he asks him what he can say why sentence of death should not be passed on him. And were He who is not willing that any should perish, but wherever He condemns 'condemns reluctant,' so to deal with us, what should we say to excuse our sins and escape their punishment? If the plea avails, we save ourselves; otherwise we cannot. Now men make excuses to their conscience, and also to their fellow-men; but let us try what value these would have at the judgment-seat of a righteous God.

First, They plead sorrow. But though their sorrow were as deep, and true, and godly, as their continuing in sin proves it is not, of what worth is this plea in the eye of the law? Some wretch by his crimes brings himself to the bar of his country—and there, pale, and sorrowful, and sad enough many have looked—but, though he pleads for his life with tears, sorrow never baulked the gallows of its due. Waste and riotous living have brought many to bankruptcy, but sorrow never satisfied the demands of defrauded and indignant creditors. Sorrow acquits no criminals: sorrow pays no debts : sorrow heals no wounds: it never restored to injured woman her fair name and character, nor recalled to life the dead, whose gray hairs a prodigal had brought down to the grave. Sorrow cannot repair the wrongs we do to our fellow-creatures, still less those we do to God. 'Offer it now to thy governor, will he be pleased with thee, or accept thy person? saith the Lord of hosts.'

Second, They plead that they have not been great sinners. This was the Pharisee's plea—'I thank thee, O God, that I am not as other men, nor even as this publican.' What that was worth, we know from this, that the poor publican, who stood afar off, and beat on his breast, and cried, 'God be merciful to me a sinner,' went down to his house justified; but not the other. The

Pharisee's was not Paul's plea. Glorying only in the cross of Christ, he called himself the least of saints, and the chief of sinners. Nor is it a plea to which any court of justice would attach the slightest value. Think of a man found guilty of theft pleading that he should be allowed to go free, because, when he stole your purse, he did not take your life! Worthless anywhere, such a plea is nowhere so worthless as at the bar where Divine justice sits enthroned; and all who reject the Saviour, rejecting mercy, shall be tried by a law whose stern terms are these, 'Cursed is every one who continueth not in all things written in the book of the law to do them.'

Third, They plead the strength of temptation. This plea, like the others—a refuge of lies, is neither new nor true. It is not true; for who can deny having committed many sins they might have avoided: yielded to many temptations they might have resisted? It is not new; having been tried in Eden, and found wanting. 'Hast thou,' said God to Adam, 'eaten of the tree whereof I commanded thee that thou shouldst not eat?' To excuse himself, he pleaded temptation—'The woman whom thou gavest to be with me, she gave me of the tree, and I did eat.' 'What is this that thou hast done?' said God, turning next to Eve. Taking up the same ground, she also pleads temptation as her excuse—'The serpent beguiled me, and I did eat.' Vain subterfuge; Eden was lost, and our world buried in the ruins of the fall! Now the plea which did not excuse their sin will still less excuse ours. For however we may plead its strength, there is no temptation we might not resist—in the hottest furnace walk unhurt, and go dryshod through the deepest sea. 'My grace is sufficient for thee,' is God's own sure and blessed word; and however hard the fight or heavy the burden, we had but to seek His grace, to boast with His servant, Paul—'I can do all things through Christ, which strengtheneth me.' Never has it been for want of faithfulness on His part, but of faith on ours, that this His grand promise has seemed to fail—'When thou passest through the waters, I will be with thee; and through the rivers, they shall not overflow thee: when thou walkest through the fire, thou shalt not be burned; neither shall the flame kindle upon thee.'

Fourth, We are of ourselves unable to embrace the salvation which God has provided. 'Believe in the Lord Jesus Christ, and thou shalt be saved,' is indeed glad tidings; but faith itself is the gift of God. Some, it is true, fancy that it is an easy thing to believe, and that we can turn our minds, as our steps when they have brought us to the brink of a precipice—turn our hearts, as the steersman the ship, which, by a prompt movement of the helm, he guides clear of the thundering reef, and sends away in safety, ploughing through the foam, on another tack. But a lost sinner—whose proper figure is a vessel without masts or rudder, drifting at the mercy of the wild waves on a rocky shore—has no power of his own to turn from sin and the error of his ways. Were it otherwise, our Lord's words had been literally, universally fulfilled—'I, if I be lifted up, will draw all men after me.' Are they so? Alas! in how many churches is He lifted up every Sabbath, nor draws one?—offered every Sabbath only to be wickedly rejected?—his servants, grieved at man's mad obstinacy, returning to their Master with the old sorrowful complaint, 'No man hath believed my report, and to none is the arm of the Lord revealed!' Could man change his heart and habits, it is incredible that any should perish with God's word in their hands; not as certainly, but more certainly, than such as never had the offer of a Saviour. Here is a man who knows that if he goes to Christ, he will go to heaven; and if not, that he shall be sent to hell—who knows that Jesus is *the way*, the only way to true happiness and holiness in this world, and salvation in the next—who knows that he must die, and that in the hour of robustest health, there is but a step between him and the grave— who knows, therefore, that if he put off salvation for a single hour, that hour may be a whole eternity too late—when, with all those powerful motives to turn this moment to Christ, that man stands unmoved, how true the words of Jesus, 'No man can come unto me except the Father which hath sent me draw him!'

No doubt, it is in the power of all, after a fashion, to use the means of grace—by that I mean to read the Bible, and say their prayers, and go to church. But, oh, what need for prayer that a Divine power may accompany these, since, without the influences of the Holy Spirit, they will be found to harden rather than to soften the heart! Experience proves this; and that he is less likely to be saved who has sat from childhood under a Gospel ministry, than one on whose eyes 'the glorious Gospel of the blessed God' opens with the novelty, and freshness, and astonishment, a man, born and brought up in a coal-pit, would feel when gazing for the first time on the star-spangled sky. Wesley and Whitefield reaped their largest harvests on neglected fields;—those, adown whose begrimed cheeks, as they preached, the starting tears ran white channels, being miners and peasants and colliers, men who heard the terrors of hell and the love of God, for the first time in their lives, set fully and affectionately before them. The heart grows callous through unsanctified familiarity with Divine things—even with danger itself. And thus, as the veteran of many a battle-field waits the advance of the foe and the crush of musketry with a calm, intrepid bearing, in like manner familiarity with spiritual danger begets such spiritual indifference that the law thunders and a Saviour entreats in vain—making it evident that men are no more to be driven from sin by the fear of hell, than drawn from it by the hopes of heaven. Put this to the test. Let the subjects of our experiment be a little child and an old man. How easy it is to awaken the fears, and touch the conscience, and bring tears to the eyes of childhood! But those only who have tried it, as I have done, can know, and those only who know it can believe, how difficult it is to reach the conscience and shake the confidence of graceless and gray-haired age. I am not depreciating the means of grace. Far from it. On the contrary, I recommend a diligent, but a devout, use of them, with earnest prayer that through an outpouring of the Holy Spirit the means may be made the channels of grace. Without that, the church we attend, and the sermons we hear, and the Bible we read, and the sacraments we partake of, will but harden our hearts—even as familiarity with funerals is apt to make us think not more but less of death, until, often treading that path which others shall one day tread with us, we can carry a neighbour to the gates of another world, and leave him there, to return to the business and pleasures of this without one suitable and serious thought.

In closing this chapter let me remark, The deeper our sense of man's inability to save himself, we are the more likely to be saved. Do not despair. Deliverance is often nearest when it seems most distant. 'Man's extremity is God's opportunity,' is one true proverb 'The darkest hour is before the dawn,' is another: and many a poor, distressed sinner's experience has been that of a crew tossed for long days on the stormy deep. They had lost their reckoning; enveloped in an impenetrable mist, their poor bark was driving they knew not where: at length they catch the dreaded roar of breakers; louder and louder they are heard thundering on a rugged shore. Unable to do anything to save themselves and avert a fatal issue, their hearts sink within them, when suddenly, as if God's own hand had drawn aside the curtain, the fog-bank parts to show them a spacious harbour, opening out its arms to receive them on the bosom of its calm blue waters. So the hope of Christ has opened to many who, finding that they had no hope in themselves, were crying, 'Sirs, what must I do to be saved?' A paradox though it seems, there is greatest hope when our case looks most hopeless. 'The Lord,' it is said, 'shall judge his people, and repent himself for his servants when he seeth that their power is gone, and that there is none shut up or left.' So it fell out with Abraham. Not till he and Isaac had climbed the mountain, not till the altar was built and the victim bound, not till with a last long look, and a last warm kiss, and a last sad farewell, the father had raised his arm to strike, was that arm arrested—did the angel, hovering over the scene, descend to stay the bloody sacrifice. It was so likewise when Israel was captive in the land of Babylon, and their harps hung mute on its willow trees, and God's own holy house lay in desolate, silent ruins. Their deliverance never seemed farther distant than when most near. Never was their captivity more galling, their misery so insulted, or their humiliation so complete, as on that night, when Belshazzar, mad with wine and wickedness, called for the vessels of the sanctuary, and turning them into drinking cups, caroused with his wives and concubines, his princes and his lords. Yet that was the very night on which the tyrant's doom was written, and the deliverance of the captives begun. Israel by the shores of the Red Sea; the three Hebrew martyrs in the fiery furnace; Daniel cast into the lions' den; Peter in chains and asleep in prison—these cases, all admirable correctives to despair, show us how God often waits till things are at the worst. He saves at the uttermost—when with all power all pride is gone. Nor shall these words have been written in vain, if any of my readers, convinced of their inability to save themselves, shall turn to Christ —like the disciples when, abandoning all further effort to keep their boat afloat and reach the land, they threw up their oars, to throw themselves on the power and love of Jesus, and wake Him with the cry, 'Master, carest thou not that we perish?' Now He does care that we should not perish. He died that we might not perish. And He who died for us, with love time can neither change nor cool, longs to save us. His arms open to embrace us. Heaven opens to admit us. Angels stand ready to rejoice over us. So venturing, as well we may, on Christ's boundless power and boundless kindness, let us fall at His feet to cry, 'Lord, save me, I perish!'—or with the man of old, 'Lord, I believe; help thou mine unbelief!'—for whosoever cometh unto Him, He will in no wise cast out; and whosoever believeth in Him shall not perish, but have everlasting life.

V.

GOD'S GIFT TO MAN.

HAS it ever occurred to the reader to mark, in almost numberless passages in the Bible, the half-magical power of the little word 'but'? Like an enchanter's wand, it suddenly turns light to darkness, or darkness to light; makes the dweller in dust to awake and sing, or fills the festive hall with horror, as if a handwriting from heaven had appeared on the wall. After considerable trouble, King David's plot against Uriah succeeds at last; the impracticable soldier will appear no more in Jerusalem; Bathsheba is brought to the palace; and amid the festivity and gladness of a royal wedding, the ugly parts of the business seem in a fair way to be forgotten. Suddenly, however, as we read the history, the whole scene is bathed in gloom; a portentous darkness comes down,—all at the bidding of the word 'but,' which demands the insertion of a little extra clause in the narrative—'B*UT* the thing that David had done displeased the Lord.' In another place we have a striking sketch of a Syrian warrior—a picture of a prosperous man into which every brilliant colour seems to enter. 'Now Naaman, captain of the host of the king of Syria, was a great man with his master, and honourable, because by him the Lord had given deliverance unto Syria; he was also a mighty man of valour.' At this point, however, the painter seems suddenly to dip his brush in ink, and dash it remorselessly against the brilliant colouring; and in our English Bible it is at the bidding of the same little word the sudden change is made—'BUT he was a leper.' In the concise forms of the Hebrew tongue it is not even necessary to express the 'but.' The contrast is marked by the single word, 'a leper;' standing in its naked expressiveness at the close of the gorgeous description, it needs no disjunctive particle to indicate the change of view; no more than if you were to describe a man as being in the best of health, and after dwelling elaborately on the healthy state of every organ, were to add in a moment that he had just swallowed a dose of deadly poison.

The most striking cases, however, of the talisman-power of the word 'but' in our Bible, are those in which man's state as a sinner is contrasted with his state of salvation through Christ. 'O Israel, thou hast destroyed thyself; BUT in me is thy help.' 'The wages of sin is death; BUT the gift of God is eternal life through Jesus Christ our Lord.' 'These shall go away into everlasting punishment, BUT the righteous into life eternal.' 'At that time ye were without Christ, being aliens from the commonwealth of Israel, and strangers to the covenants of promise, having no hope, and without God in the world. BUT now, in Christ Jesus, ye who sometimes were far off are made nigh by the blood of

Christ.' Perhaps the most remarkable instance of any occurs in the beginning of the second chapter of Ephesians. Nothing can be blacker than the picture drawn there of the natural condition of the members of that church. They were dead in trespasses and sins. Dead, however, in a sense that implied neither rest nor peace, because they were possessed and driven by lusts of evil and spirits of darkness, that, like the devils in the herd of swine, were forcing them to the brink of a terrible precipice. The first three verses of the chapter (omitting the words in italics, '*hath he quickened*,' in the first verse, which at that place rather hurt the sense than improve it) are a dramatic representation of this frightful scene. A host of human beings, blind and ghastly as corpses, are hurrying tumultuously along, impelled by wild, infernal impulses, down a steep place to the edge of the gulf. Their doom seems inevitable, they are rushing at such a pace and with such momentum, that no power on earth can save them. Suddenly, however an arm is stretched out from heaven. Man's extremity is God's opportunity. As though it were in a dissolving view, the picture of wild tumult and ghastly ruin gives place all of a sudden to one of heavenly life and tranquillity. And the change is again introduced by the same magical word: 'BUT God, who is rich in mercy, for his great love wherewith he loved us, even when we were dead in sins, hath quickened us together with Christ.'

There can be little doubt that these frequent and striking contrasts of the two states are introduced in Scripture on purpose; and a slight measure of reflection will show to any intelligent reader what that purpose must be.

1. Thus, in the first place, they make it very plain that the two states are essentially *separate* from each other—the state of sin and the state of grace in Christ.

But for such remarkable contrasts we might suppose—what at all times we are prone enough to do—that there is no great difference between the one state and the other; that men differ from each other, or differ from their former selves, only in this, that in some there is more evil and less good, and in others more good and less evil. We might suppose that the only distinction between men, in a moral sense, lay in the proportions in which good and evil entered into their character, and that as these proportions are all but infinitely varied, so their classification must be equally diversified, and that no hard division of men into two great states, or into two great classes, would even be practicable. But abounding as the Bible does with the sharp contrasts we have referred to, such a view cannot be held. The testimony of Scripture is explicit that there are just two grand states—a state of sin and a state of grace, a state of death and a state of life. No doubt many difficult questions arise out of this doctrine. On these it were wise for us to leave the veil of obscurity as it is left in the Bible; but that this is the doctrine of the Bible can hardly be denied. And who does not see how thoroughly this view is borne out by the personal teaching of Christ himself? What feature of that teaching is so remarkable as the division of his hearers into two great classes? The two gates, the wide and the strait; the two ways, the broad and the narrow; the twofold terminus, destruction and life; the two kinds of builders, on the rock and on the sand; the two classes of virgins, those with oil in their lamps and those without oil; the wheat and the chaff; the branches for fruit and the branches for fuel; and, to mention but one other, the grand division on the great day of judgment of the sheep and the goats, the striking contrasts brought out between the lives of the two classes, and the awful solemnity of the Judge's sole alternative, 'Come, ye blessed,' or 'Depart, ye cursed,' —all show the prominence of this grand division in the mind of Christ, and the vast pains he took to leave a clear and most solemn impression of it on the hearts of all who heard Him.

2. Another purpose of these striking contrasts is to show clearly that sinful man cannot be his own Saviour.

In all ages his tendency has been to believe in his ability to save himself. In no age of the world was this tendency ever more strong than it is in some quarters at the present day. We should remark, however, that the word *save* is not a proper word in such a connection. Wherever man holds himself sufficient, or nearly sufficient, to remedy the evils of his condition, he cannot believe that he is lost, and it is only the lost that need to be saved. It is but some spots of dust he has got on his garments, some slight dislocations his machinery has undergone, some stupid errors into which he has ignorantly fallen, or which have been handed down from his fathers, and out of which education and experience will by-and-by be sure to extricate him. And so there are men in our day, of highest culture and scholarship too, who have discovered that there is no need for God to help human creatures up the heights of improvement—nay, that there is no such being as a personal God at all! The gospel of these men, according to their most recent oracle, 'is the gospel of αὐτάρκεια, the creed of self-sufficience, which sees for man no clearer or deeper duty than that of intellectual self-reliance, self-dependence, self-respect — an evangel not to be cancelled or supplanted by any revelation of mystic, or prophet, or saint.' This is the boldest utterance that the spirit of self-dependence has ever yet given out. It is needless surely to remark that the self-dependence here extolled is quite unlike that healthy self-reliance which teaches a man not to depend on his fellow-creatures for anything that with God's help he can do himself. What you are here taught is, not that you are to be independent of your fellow-men, but independent even of God!

Into such a wild extreme as this, no one that reads these pages is ever likely to fall. But how prone are we to fancy, nevertheless, that to a large extent we are able to save ourselves! The debt we owe to God's justice, may we not pay at least a part of it by our penitence for the past, our increased diligence for the future, our better lives, our abounding good works? The power that sin has got in our hearts, may we not check it, and in some degree overcome it, if we are only watchful of our habits—if we are but on our guard against temptation, and earnest in our efforts to control ourselves? True, we are weak and frail: at best we come far short of perfection. But will not Christ make up for our deficiencies, and will not God by His Spirit help our infirmities? If we try to do our best, what need we fear? What more can be expected of us than that we should do what we can? How can it be supposed that a righteous God will exact impossibilities, and demand of us a perfection which we can no more give than we can fly to the stars?

To all these questions there is at least one answer. They all assume that man can more or less save himself. They assume, therefore, the opposite of what is taught by those vivid contrasts between man's state by nature and his state by grace, to which we have so often adverted. If man can be his own saviour, these contrasts have no meaning. There is no propriety in speaking of death as the wages of sin, and eternal life as the gift of God through Jesus Christ our Lord; there is no propriety in speaking of man as self-destroyed, and affirming that his only help is in God. All those passages become misleading and worse, that stop men's mouths and declare them alike guilty and helpless. But is it so? Is man sufficient for his own deliverance? Nay, let God be true, but every man a liar. Talk of doing your best—who is there that does his best? What kind of conscience can the man have who affirms that he does his best? 'If we say that we are without sin we deceive ourselves, and the truth is not in us.' And are we not responsible, too, in a large degree, for our inability, even when we try earnestly to do what we are called by God's law to do? When a school-boy has trifled away nine-tenths of the time allotted for preparing a lesson, when he has wasted his strength and dissipated his mental energies in some exciting sport, and then, hurrying at the last moment to his task, strives without effect to overtake it, is it excuse enough that he is *then* doing his best? Was he not to blame for wasting the rest of the time? Was he not to blame for letting his attention be diverted and his energies scattered, so that he could not concentrate them on his task when at length he tried? And is there no blame to be attached to man in like manner for his inability to obey God's law, even when he makes the effort? Is not this in great part the fruit of the inattention, and the trifling, and the self-indulgence, and the worldliness of his past life? Sufficiently so, at least, to justify his condemnation? It may often be hard to admit this. It is always hard to give up the idea of saving ourselves. It is hard for a merchant to admit that he is a bankrupt, and to lie down at the feet of his creditors. It is hard for a sinner to admit that he is a bankrupt before God, and cast himself, without one plea of his own, on the Divine mercy. But, if we would ever taste the sweets of salvation, we must submit to this act of humiliation. Adam must give up his miserable apron of fig-leaves, if his shame is ever to be covered. All of us must abandon our filthy rags, if we are to wear the white robe of salvation. We must give up the notion that we are rich and increased with goods, and have need of nothing, and admit that we are wretched, and miserable, and poor, and blind, and naked.

3. Our next remark is already obvious: the contrasts of which we are speaking are designed to bring out very clearly that man's salvation proceeds wholly from the mercy and love of God.

It is an act of pure grace, not only not deserved, but the very opposite of what is deserved. It is a blessed present to one who deserved a signal punishment: 'the wages of sin is death, but eternal life is the gift of God through Jesus Christ our Lord.' No words could be more fitly chosen to convey the truth, that so far as man is concerned, his case is hopeless; and that his salvation is due solely to the generosity and grace of God. So, also, in another of the passages already quoted, where out of the chaos and confusion of his self-caused ruin a hand from heaven is stretched out to save. 'GOD, who is *rich in mercy*, for his *great love* wherewith he loved us.' Geographers tell us that many of our greatest rivers, such as the Euphrates and the Tigris, have a twofold source. The same is true of the river of the water of life. It originates in these two fountains, the 'mercy' and the 'love' of God. And these fountains are not meagre and precarious streamlets, for He is '*rich* in mercy,' and it is a '*great* love wherewith he loved us.' 'For God *so* loved the world, that he gave his only-begotten Son, that whosoever believeth in him should not perish, but should have everlasting life.' The boundless *compassion* of God pitied the children of men, as He saw them led by Satan, ridden by sin, exiles from home, slaves to corruption, blindfolded by the world, cut off from heaven, and bound for hell. And the boundless *love* of God has devised a method of salvation at a cost and sacrifice to Himself that no words can tell, or figures calculate, adapted to remedy every evil that sin has introduced, offered as a free gift to all men, without money and without price, if only they will take it *as a gift,* and acknowledge the infinite mercy that has thus changed them from children of wrath and heirs of hell to children of God and heirs of glory.

There are many misconceptions of God's attitude towards sinners, which this view of the origin of salvation is fitted to remove. Let us just glance at two. In the first place it sweeps away the conception that God is an easy-minded Being, who looks with considerable indifference on the delinquencies of sinners, and now that Christ has suffered for them, is more than ever disposed to treat them with indulgence and leniency. If there be any feeling more remote than another from that which the Scriptures ascribe to God in connection with man's sin, it is that of easy-minded indifference. The infinite depths of

God's nature are stirred by man's sin. No wonder! · Man, the crown and glory of creation, is stained from head to foot with the abominable thing which He hates; he who alone of earthly creatures was made in His image, is impregnated through and through with the quality which is too disgusting for Him to look on. Never was such intense compassion known as that which surges in the Divine bosom when the fatal blow behoves to be struck. 'How shall I give thee up, Ephraim? how shall I deliver thee, Israel? how shall I make thee as Admah? how shall I set thee as Zeboim? Mine heart is turned within me, my repentings are kindled together.' Never was there such pains taken with any Divine plan, or such a sacrifice made to fulfil it, as in the arrangements for the salvation of men. If it were possible for God to be easy-minded, to make large allowance for sinners, to adopt a policy of indulgence, to wink at the iniquity of his children, why make such a work about their guilt, and about their redemption? If the whole subject of man's sin could be easily left to the mere mercy of God, why should God Himself manifest such intense emotion in connection with it, and why should such a price be paid for his ransom as the blood of the only-begotten Son?

The other misconception of God's attitude towards sinners, is that which represents Him as full of wrath and fury against them, pursuing them, so to speak, like the avenger of blood, like Saul enraged at David, and never abating His rage, till His own Son rushed between them, and received in His own person the blows and the bolts that were meant for them. It is hard to say if this view was ever deliberately given, except as an enemy's caricature of the doctrine of the atonement. But if the leaven of it should lurk in any one's mind, let it be for ever expelled by the consideration that salvation is God's gift to sinners; that the stream of the water of life has its origin in the rich mercy and great love of the Father; that, so far from thirsting for the sinner's punishment, God's very soul shrunk from inflicting it; that all the three Persons of the Godhead are one in their feelings toward the human family; and that 'there is joy in heaven over one sinner that repenteth.' And if anything more should be needed to expel the idea of God's eagerness to hurl His thunderbolts at the sinner, let it be considered that the feeling thus ascribed to God is one of the most wretched weaknesses of fallen humanity. There are two grounds, utterly different from each other, on which displeasure may be felt at an offence. On the one hand, you may be grieved and horrified at the sin itself, and if you be a judge, whose duty it is to punish the guilty, you will be much distressed at the necessity of inflicting retribution for a deed so wicked. On the other hand, you may care little or nothing about the criminality of the act, or the guilt of the offender, but may be greatly exasperated and provoked at the annoyance or injury *done to yourself*. Alas, the wrath of many at the sins of others has no higher source than this! You may have as many sins and vices as you please, without rousing their emotion in any shape, so long as you do not come across their path; but the moment you annoy or injure them, there is no bound to their indignation, or to their eagerness to punish and restrain you. But how selfish and unholy is the indignation that is inspired solely by such a cause as this! To ascribe any such feeling to God is not merely to make Him a partner of our infirmities, but a partaker of our meanest sins. How different the quality of that wrath which burns in His holy bosom! The passage which we have quoted so often shows clearly how *such wrath exists alongside of infinite mercy and infinite love.* The description of the state of the Ephesians has reached its climax when they are called 'children of wrath, even as others.' God's 'wrath' was their very heritage, the element in which they lived, the mother, it might almost appear, of whom they were born. Yet at the same moment, as we read in the very next clause, they were the objects of God's rich mercy and wonderful love.

What marvellous combinations of feeling the Divine heart can cherish! Constant and burning wrath side by side with infinite compassion and love! 'For my ways are not your ways, neither are your thoughts my thoughts, saith the Lord. For as the heaven is higher than the earth, so are my ways higher than your ways, and my thoughts than your thoughts.'

One other purpose of these contrasts we mention—to set forth the completeness and glory of God's salvation.

There are contrasts of colour, familiar to every artist, which are always made use of when it is designed to give great force and prominence to some figure or object in a picture. The deeper the gloom of the heavens behind, the brighter seems the flash of lightning that throws a moment of midday into the darkness of the night. So also the glory of God's salvation is made to appear greater when it is placed side by side with the picture of man's ruin. It is a favourite practice of some of the sacred writers to place the two together. In the prophets we sometimes find awful pictures of guilt, and when we might expect these to be followed by tremendous denunciations of punishment, we find them actually followed by magnificent manifestations of mercy. The first chapter of Isaiah is one of the darkest in all the Bible; its first words are an impassioned appeal to earth and heaven against those whom God had nourished and brought up as children, but who had rebelled against Him. As it proceeds it advances fresh charges, and detects in their most sacred services the abominations of hypocrisy in place of the beauties of holiness; and then, at the very climax, when you might have expected a burst of thunder, you have a burst of mercy— 'Come now, and let us reason together, saith the Lord: though your sins be as scarlet, they shall be as white as snow; though they be red like crimson, they shall be as wool.' So also, to take but one more instance, in the twenty-eighth chapter of the same prophet; the 'scornful men' that rule Jerusalem are arraigned for their matchless wickedness, and after many a remonstrance with them for particular forms of sin, the head and front of their offending is set forth in these startling words—'Because ye have said, We have made a covenant with death, and with hell are we at agreement; when the overflowing scourge shall pass through, it shall not come unto us: for we have made lies our refuge, and under falsehood have we hid ourselves.' What then? What follows such outrageous wickedness? Does the earth open her mouth, or hell her jaws, to ingulf them? The very reverse! 'Therefore thus saith the Lord God, Behold, I lay in Zion for a foundation a stone, a tried stone, a precious corner stone; a sure foundation: he that believeth shall not make haste.' But to guard against the abuse of this matchless grace it is added—'Judgment also will I lay to the line, and righteousness to the plummet: and the hail shall sweep away the refuge of lies, and the waters shall overflow the hiding-place.'

Thus does God impressively show us the completeness and the glory of His salvation. He places it side by side with the evil which it is designed to remedy, and however terrible may be the aspect of the one, it is dissipated like vapour by the glory of the other. The remedy has not been devised on a superficial and cursory view of the evil that has to be provided for; that evil has been surveyed in every aspect, and gauged in every dimension; and still the result is, that 'where sin abounded, grace does much more abound.' The gift of God is not a mere palliation that will but modify some of the features of the disease, it is a glorious remedy that will search it to its depths till not a trace of it remains. No doubt it is a strong man in whose arms the sinner lies bound and helpless; but He who has come to bind him is infinitely stronger! Delightful and blessed assurance! If it be terrible to think how we are children of disobedience and children of wrath—how we are environed by sin and death and hell—how these hold us in a vice, like the grim serpents that held Laocoon and his sons in their inextricable folds, it is glorious to think of One beside us, at whose word all the powers of darkness let go their hold, and who, if we will but grasp His hand, will bring us out into the glorious liberty of the sons of God. But ever let us remember, that as is the privilege, so also is the responsibility; and that just because the salvation is so complete and so glorious, so also is the doom of those who reject it hopeless and ir-remediable. *'How shall we escape, if we neglect so great salvation?'*

VI.

THE SAVIOUR'S PERSON.

THERE are different ways of making a present. When it is such a thing as money, or bread, or clothing, it is not only given, but given away by the giver, and not only taken, but taken away by the receiver. Such things are enjoyed apart from the person from whom they come; sometimes, indeed, with grateful remembrances of his kindness, but quite as often amid thankless indifference and thoughtless neglect. But gifts may be offered in a different form. A benevolent man, touched by the ignorance of a community, may make them a present of a teacher, or touched by their ailments, a present of a doctor; that is, he may provide for the maintenance of such persons, and arrange with them to labour in the district. Or better still, he himself may settle among the people, and devote his whole time and energy to the task of removing their ignorance and relieving their sufferings. In this case, the present, though given, is not given away, and the benefit, while taken, is not taken away. By the nature of the case the present is connected with the person of the donor, and the benefaction depends on personal intercourse with him. Those who wish to get the benefit must come into a direct and friendly relation to him : and, supposing him to be perfectly qualified for his work, the degree of benefit they receive will depend on the amount of respect they cherish for his person, the eagerness with which they receive his instructions, and the heartiness with which they commit themselves to his guidance.

It is much more after the latter of these methods than the former that God makes his great gift to men. 'This is the record, that God hath given to us eternal life, *and this life is in* his Son.' (1 John v. 11.) All that enters into the composition of eternal life, God's gift to sinners, has been committed in the first instance to the Son. All the qualifications for procuring it centre in Him; the work to be done for it was done by Him; and all the blessings it consists of are stored or deposited in Him. If we would have eternal life, therefore, we must come into personal communication with the Son. He gives it, but He does not give it away. If we would take it, we cannot take it away. We must take it by receiving Christ in whom it subsists, partly in the same way as the Hebrews in Egypt could obtain deliverance only by receiving Moses, the appointed deliverer. They had a distinct promise of deliverance and national life, but when the time came for its fulfilment, it was found to be inseparably connected with the person of Moses. To reject Moses was to reject deliverance; to receive Moses, and give all due honour to him and to his messages, was the way to salvation. So for us, likewise, to receive Christ, is to secure life; to reject Christ, is to reject life. 'For he that believeth on the Son hath everlasting life; and he that believeth not the Son shall not see life; but the wrath of God abideth on him.'

Two grand inquiries fall to be made respecting Christ, viewed as the Being in whom eternal life subsists for the benefit and salvation of men. The first inquiry has respect to his *person*, the second to his *work*. Who is He, and what has He done? What assurance does the nature of the case afford to the mind and conscience of man, that He is qualified to bestow the life which He offers, and that in closing with His offer, and committing ourselves to His guidance, we shall be conducted to those realms of glory which our wistful hearts sometimes dream of, as some captive soldier in a lonely dungeon may dream of the festive gatherings of his youth, as of scenes which it were almost, and yet not quite, vain to hope ever to see again.

It is to the testimony of God's word we must look for our guidance on both these questions. Reason, by herself, is quite unable to thread her way through the darkness and difficulties of such inquiries, and even when the lamp of Revelation is employed to light our path, we are compelled again and again to hold up our hands in amazement, and to say, 'Great is the mystery of godliness!'

That a great mystery attaches to the *person* of Christ, according to the received view of it, every one will surely allow. The union of the two natures, finite and infinite, in one person, transcends the compass of our faculties, and when we try to fathom the subject we find ourselves 'in wandering mazes lost.' If our spirit be humble and child-like as it ought to be, we shall be content to believe where we cannot hope to comprehend, and willing to adore at the base of heights to whose cloud-capped summits we dare not, in this life at all events, think of climbing.

So also, although some are less ready to acknowledge it, there is a mystery about Christ's work. The fancy of some is, that in this department all can be made clear and level to an ordinary capacity; that all about that righteousness which is like the great mountains, and those judgments which are a great deep—all about the relation of the Judicial to the Paternal, all about atonement, satisfaction, and reconciliation, can be made as plain as a rule of arithmetic! Surely it is wise to believe that a shade of mystery must lie upon the work as well as upon the person of the Saviour. It is wise for us to believe this, while firmly repudiating the opposite error that everything about the work is involved in impenetrable obscurity. 'We know in part' indeed, but we do know a part. Let us be content with the part we may know. There are glorious things revealed concerning the work of Christ, enough to assure the most rigid conscience that every demand of divine righteousness is satisfied in it, and that the acceptance of the sinner for Christ's sake is not more subservient to his welfare than to God's glory. But for the most part, what the Bible brings before us is the simple fact that 'Christ hath once suffered for sin, the just for the unjust, to bring us unto God.' And the chief texts that in all ages and communions have brought peace and joy to stricken sinners, that have been like lamps from heaven to numberless death-beds, are those which set forth the work of Christ in its simplest and broadest aspect—'Behold the Lamb of God that taketh away the sin of the world;' 'Him that cometh unto me I will in no wise cast out;' 'The blood of Jesus Christ his Son cleanseth us from all sin.'

If we follow the light of Scripture on the subject of Christ's person, we shall find these three things taught concerning it:—First, that Jesus Christ is the Eternal Son of God; second, that He became man; and third, that He was both God and Man in One Person, and will so remain for evermore.

1. Jesus Christ is the Eternal Son of God. The most cursory reader of the Bible must see that, according to its teaching, Jesus Christ is the Son of God in a sense in which no other being is His son. He is the 'only begotten Son, who is

in the bosom of the Father.' So peculiar is His claim, and so unique is the relation, that as God is emphatically called ' *The* Father,' so Jesus is as emphatically called ' *The* Son.' ' Whatsoever ye shall ask THE FATHER in my name, that will He do, that THE FATHER may be glorified in THE SON.' The doctrine established by this very remarkable mode of expression is that of the 'Eternal Sonship.' It is a doctrine that may be said to flow from God's Fatherhood. If God be eternally the Father, He must have eternally a Son. There cannot be a father without a son, and there cannot be an eternal father without an eternal son. It is the property of the Father eternally to beget, and the property of the Son to be eternally begotten. The subject is awfully mysterious. St Augustine tried to bring it a step nearer to us by a simple illustration. He supposed a lake to have existed from eternity, with a flower on its margin, and a light falling on the flower. The flower in that case must eternally have had a shadow. It is the property of the flower eternally to produce the shadow, and the property of the shadow to be eternally produced by the flower. Such was St Augustine's faint attempt to illustrate a relation of which no adequate conception is possible to us, certainly not in the life that now is, and it may be not even in that which is to come.

Two things, however, may be noted concerning this relation—one as to what it does not imply, the other as to what it does.

' It implies *no inferiority*. The Son is not inferior to the Father. He is the same in substance, equal in power and glory. He is the brightness of His glory, and the express image of His person. He is uncreated Light of uncreated Light, very God of very God, the Alpha and the Omega, the First and the Last. The seraphim in His presence veil their faces and their feet, crying, ' Holy, holy, holy, Lord God of hosts.' Like the Father, He dwells in light inaccessible and full of glory. The angels worship Him as they worship the Father. His voice, equally with the Father's, summons the things that are not into being. And like the Father, He is separated from the highest angel by a gulf infinitely wider than that which separates the highest angel from the meanest insect—the gulf, in a word, that separates the creature from the Creator, the finite from the Infinite, the child of yesterday from the Eternal God.

The other thing to be remarked of this relation is, that it implies great tenderness and gladsomeness of feeling. It invests the fellowship of the First and Second Persons with the indescribable charm of kinship, the kinship which subsists between a father and his son. It is not easy to define, even in the case of a human relationship, the nature of that peculiar joy which kinship adds to the fellowship of congenial hearts. It is, of course, far more difficult to comprehend the nature or the force of this element in the case of Divine Persons. But of the reality of it we have some remarkable glimpses. Where is the Son's characteristic place? In the bosom of the Father. What is the Father's feeling to the Son?

'Behold my servant whom I uphold, mine elect in whom my soul delighteth!' If paternal feelings dispose to a more tender, protecting love, they must have had this effect in the case of God. And this makes it the more wonderful that He should have given up His Son to agony and death to take away the sins of the world, and gives an unanswerable emphasis to that challenge of the Apostle, 'He that spared not his own Son, but delivered Him up for us all, how shall he not with Him also freely give us all things?'

2. The next great fact taught us as to the person of Christ is, that He became man. He took to Himself a true body and a reasonable soul. He became a true brother of our race, bone of our bone, and flesh of our flesh; was acquainted with all our human feelings—our sorrows, and weaknesses, and trials—all but sin. The Scriptures, while they are so explicit in affirming Christ's proper Divinity, are at equal pains in affirming and illustrating His true humanity. He entered

the world as we enter it, for He was born; He left the world as we leave it, for He died. And no little care is taken to fill up these, the great outlines of His human life. We have the picture of the young mother, weary and travel-worn, reaching Bethlehem in much the same condition as Rachel had approached it centuries before; taking refuge in the stable, bringing forth her babe there, wrapping Him in swaddling bands, and laying Him in the manger. We are told of the flight into Egypt, caused by the cruel plot against His life, for even His life had to be protected by the same contrivances as ours. We have His return to Nazareth, where He was subject to His parents, and His growth in stature and in wisdom, and in favour with God and with man. We have the incident of His being lost at Jerusalem, and the picture of the commotion when that loss became known, just as there would be in any of our own households if one of our children was lost; we read of the mother's joy, and the mother's impatience too, on finding

Him; and lest we should forget His Divinity amid such multiplied tokens of His humanity, we have the wonderful reply to His mother—the solitary floweret, as it has been called, from the enclosed garden of the thirty years—'Wist ye not that I must be about my Father's business?' In riper years we see Him in all the ordinary conditions in which the poorer class of men are found: wearied with heat and travel, sitting on a well; wearied with work and teaching, retiring for rest to the quiet hills, or putting off in a boat to be refreshed by the cool lake-breeze; we see Him eating, drinking, hungering, thirsting, sleeping, sorrowing, rejoicing, praying, shuddering, weeping. We see Him shrinking from agony and death, as we too shrink from them, then bracing Himself to meet them, and going forth in defiance of them, clad in divine armour and strong in divine strength. We see Him on the cross, committing His poor mother to the care of a humble disciple, expressing the common sensation of dying humanity, 'I thirst'—uttering

His last word, drawing His last breath, when His head droops as ours would droop, and He gives up the ghost. What a mystery is this incarnation, and yet what an undeniable fact! Is it not true that many excellent Christians think of it too little, go too seldom to the cradle of Jesus? True, there *is* an overwhelming attraction to the cross. The cross speaks to us of completed redemption, of an everlasting and all-sufficient righteousness, and when our souls are agitated by guilt and conscious unworthiness, its voice comes to us like the words of Jesus over the Sea of Galilee, 'Peace, be still.' But if Calvary has its overwhelming attraction, Bethlehem has its attraction too. That stable is a wonderful school for faith and joy, and has lessons that make it good for us to be there. It teaches us that for evermore the life of Jesus has been poured into the current of our human life, that the Eternal Son has joined Himself to us for ever, that on our dishonoured escutcheon the Prince of Heaven has quartered His arms, never to be effaced. O fact, full of hope and blessing ! O Elder Brother, thou wilt not cast off any of Thy brethren when they come to Thee, bedraggled and tattered though their garments be, and though their hearts and lives be defiled a thousand times worse ! Strong Son of Man, Thou wilt not leave any fallen and crawling member of Thy race who looks wistfully to Thee, till Thou hast brought him among the many sons to glory, till Thou hast washed him, and cleansed him through the washing of water by the word ; and till Thou hast presented him to Thyself a member of Thy glorious Church, without spot or wrinkle or any such thing !

Let us mark another fact, too, both in the incarnation and the death of Jesus. In the life of every human being, the two things that are most beyond his control are his birth and his death. Except in the case of those who sinfully or insanely take their death into their own hands, no choice is afforded us ; we can but bow to our destiny in the one and in the other. In the case of Jesus, on the other hand, both His birth and His death, and all the circumstances attending them, were subject to His own calm determination. He willed to be born, and He willed to die, knowing the humiliation and sufferings attending each. He willed to be born among the beasts at Bethlehem; He willed to die amid thieves and fiends at Calvary!

3. *Jesus was and continues to be both God and man for ever.* It is not necessary here to do more than allude in passing to various other views that have been held on the person of Jesus: as, that He had only the *appearance* of a body—the error so warmly denounced by St John; that He had not a human soul, but that His divine nature was His soul; that the two natures subsisted in two persons very intimately connected; or that the two natures were blended into one compound nature, possessing the properties and qualities of both. Our doctrine is, that the two natures, with their distinct properties and qualities, belonged to Christ, yet that they made but one

personality, one being, one Christ. And this is gathered from the texts in which the same being is spoken of as both God and man, and the attributes, now of God and now of man, are ascribed to His one person. 'Feed the flock of GOD, which he hath purchased *with his own blood.*' 'I am the bread of Life.' 'I am the Resurrection and the Life.' Who made these statements? 'Is not this the carpenter's son?' asked the Jews, 'and are not his brethren with us?' Yet the carpenter's son, the same who went out one morning in search of a fig or other morsel to break His fast, claims not only to have, but to be the Bread of Life, and He who begged of the woman of Samaria a draught from Jacob's well, claims not only to have, but to be the Water of Life. It is the same *I* who on the cross says, 'I thirst,' and in the streets of Jerusalem, 'If any man thirst, let him come *unto me* and drink.' In the same *I*, the necessities of the human being and the infinite powers of the Mighty God are blended! How soon do we get beyond our depth when we occupy ourselves with such a theme! Like bathers on a sloping beach, we go out but a yard or two, and immediately we are in deep waters; or like Noah's dove, we roam hither and thither, but find no rest for the sole of our foot. After all, is it wonderful that it should be so? 'Canst thou by searching find out God; canst thou find out the Almighty unto perfection? It is high as heaven, what canst thou know; deeper than hell, what canst thou think? The measure thereof is longer than the earth and broader than the sea.' If in His unity even, God is incomprehensible, what must He not be in the Trinity of Persons? And what must He not be in the incarnation of one of these Persons, and the assumption of a creature's finite nature into union with His infinite nature in one person for ever?

But little though it be that we can understand of this great mystery, we see enough to assure us that from the wonderful constitution of His Person, Jesus Christ is amply sufficient for the work of redemption. There are cases in which a practised eye can tell beforehand whether or not a beam be equal to a weight, whether or not a back be equal to a burden. *There* is a large waggon, with goods piled heavily aloft, making no contemptible load; but *here* is a team of the strongest and noblest horses, and before they begin to pull, we know instinctively that they are able for the effort. *There* is a brawling stream, rushing through its channel of rock as if it would sweep all before it; yonder is a single plank, wasted through long exposure, so palpably frail, that you cannot think of intrusting yourself to it; but *here*, a little further down, is a strong iron bridge spanning the stream; you have not a doubt but that it is sufficient for your weight, and that you may cross in safety. *There* is the awful burden of human sin, rising up like a mountain to heaven, and defying all man's resources and skill to remove it; but *here* is One who is at once the Son of God and the Son of Man, travailing in the greatness of His might, and constraining us to say, 'Who art thou, O great mountain? Before this Zerubbabel, thou shalt be a plain.' If power, worth, and dignity be needed for the work of redemption, they are brought to the task in infinite degree by the Son of God; if sympathy, brotherhood, and a capacity of suffering be needed, they are brought in all fulness by the Son of Man. We have but to look at this Lamb of God to be convinced that He can take away the sin of the world. We have but to examine this foundation-stone, elect and precious, to see that it is fitted to bear the superstructure of the Church of the redeemed. 'Behold my servant, whom I uphold, mine elect, in whom my soul delighteth; I have put my Spirit upon him, he shall bring forth judgment to the Gentiles. . . . He shall not fail or be discouraged till he have set judgment in the earth; and the isles shall wait for his law.'

In a somewhat less exalted point of view, it is most instructive to remember that Jesus Christ was successively an infant, a child, a boy, a young man, and a man of mature strength and years. An infant, with that which is so characteristic of infancy, its utter feebleness, its helpless and absolute dependence upon others; a child, obedient to His parents, accustoming Himself to control every desire of His own, and conscientiously act in compliance with their will; a boy, and even then glad when it was said to Him, 'Let us go up to the house of the Lord,' and intent upon His Father's business; a young man, quiet, modest, unobtrusive, calmly preparing Himself for the business of His after-life; and finally a man, 'toiling, rejoicing, sorrowing,' bravely fighting life's great battles, and bent on finishing the work that was given Him to do. And He knows and understands all about these several stages of life. Let each of us lay hold of the great privilege of brotherhood with Him, claiming His sympathy and help, setting His high example before us, and aspiring to walk in His footsteps. 'For we have not an High Priest that cannot be touched with the feeling of our infirmities; but was in all points tempted like as we are, yet without sin.'

VII.

THE WORK AND GLORY OF THE SAVIOUR.

AMONG other objections which infidels have taken, but vainly taken, to the divinity of the Bible, one has been the mysteries it contained. Here, driven from one post to another, some have taken their last stand; entrenching themselves in that as in a strong and impregnable position. The Bible, they affirm, cannot be a revelation from God, because it contains unintelligible statements; doctrines which man finds it impossible to comprehend. To such an objection it would not be easy to find a more conclusive reply than the answer of a plain, humble Christian. Dexterously turning the infidel's artillery against himself, he converted his objection to the Scriptures into an argument for their truth. 'Not comprehend?' he replied; 'I would not believe the Bible to be the word of God, if it contained nothing but what I could fully comprehend!'

There is great force in this remark. For the Bible were unlike the other works of God, if it came in all respects within the grasp of our limited understandings. There are mysteries in God's works as great as any to be found in His word. Take an example. In reproaching the children of Israel for their wilful and wicked ignorance, Jeremiah exclaims, 'The stork in the heavens knoweth her appointed times, and the turtle and the crane and the swallow know the time of their coming; but my people know not the judgment of the Lord.' In birds of passage, which always travel with the sun, every summer brings us visitors from southern climes; and, as they roost amid the palm-groves of Asia, or sport on the banks of the Nile, how do they know that, in a few more days or weeks, the snows shall have melted from our fields, and ice-bound streams, set loose, will be rushing merrily to the sea, and the sun shining through long summer days on our distant isle? By what means do they know, not only when to come, but how to come? What a mystery is there! In sailing to a remote foreign land, man has to provide himself with chart and compass. Now he takes observations in the heavens, and now sounds the ocean with deep-sea lead; by day and night the steersman stands silent by the helm, and the watch tread the deck; and yet, notwithstanding all their science, and skill, and care, men often miss the desired haven, and perish, wrecked amid the angry breakers of an unknown shore. Look now at the voyage of a bird of passage! For many hundred or thousand miles it cleaves its course through the pathless air, without compass, or chart, or pilot to guide its flight; onward it goes through the wildest storms, through densest fogs, and the darkness of starless nights; yet—a fact well ascertained, but a mystery inexplicable—it returns over seas and lands and rivers and mountains to the very spot and home of its birth! What more inexplicable in the word of God than we have here? It is past finding out. How absurd, then, to make its mysteries an objection to the divinity of the Bible! If not in these things only, but in the painting of every flower, in the shaping of every leaf, in the shooting of every blade of grass—

> 'God moves in a mysterious way,
> His wonders to perform,'

need we start at finding mysteries in the great work of Redemption?—at an Apostle, as he contemplates it, holding up his hands in wonder to exclaim, 'Great is the mystery of godliness, God manifest in the flesh?' This grand mystery, the person of Him who was both God and man, we have had already under consideration; and we would now turn with believing, loving, adoring eyes to contemplate His Work and Glory.

In the cell where a captive had lain long immured, I have seen the successive days of his imprisonment scored with a nail on the naked walls—as each passed, and brought his sentence nearer to a close, he marked it off; giving God thanks that another day was gone. Alas for them who, rejecting the mercy of a gracious God, are cast into outer darkness! No such employment occupies their attention, or alleviates the misery of their lot. The crown never fades on the brow of saints—the joys at God's right hand are for evermore; and for evermore also is their doom, who, preferring their sins to Jesus, resist alike the sweet attractions of His cross and the awful terrors of His law—their worm never dieth, and their fire is never quenched.

In eternity there are neither years, nor days, nor hours; yet there have been two hours in time which are drawn out, if I may say so, over the length of eternal ages. One, that hour, pregnant of evil, when Eve, tempted of the devil, plucked the forbidden fruit, and the fall ensued. The sea wastes its fury on the shore, and after raging for a while, falls asleep like a fretful child; continents limit the range and ravages of earthquakes; the grave, where the wicked cease from troubling, and the weary are at rest, sets bounds to the power of the oppressor; but limited in its influence to no place, or age, or race of men, the shock of that fall was felt throughout all the world. Nor shall its consequences cease with the world, and with time. When this old world shall be no more, and time shall be lost in eternity, and death itself shall die, that unhappy hour shall live in the memory, and be felt in the misery of the lost.

The other hour, pregnant with greatest good, as the first was with greatest evil, to the world, one which, more than any in the whole course of ages, has occupied the attention and excited the expectations of earth, and hell, and heaven too, was that our Lord pointed at when He said, 'The hour is come when the Son of Man should be glorified.' There, as is plain from the words that follow, 'Verily, verily, except a corn of wheat fall into the ground and die, it abideth alone; but if it die, it bringeth forth much fruit,' Jesus refers to His approaching death. In that hour,

His great work, to use His own last words, was 'finished,' and the head He bowed in death was crowned with its brightest glory.

1. There were circumstances of visible glory attending our Lord's death. Apart from the spiritual blessings which flow to us from it, and apart also from the revenue of glory Christ derives from the Church, both in earth and heaven, which He has redeemed by His blood, there never was a death like His. It is as true that never man died as He died, as that never man spake as He spake. Rays of Godhead streamed through the darkest scenes of His humiliation; or lent these such splendour as the sun imparts to the edges of the murky cloud that conceals His face. Jesus was born, like any other child, but the fruit of a virgin's womb. Angels attended and celebrated with songs the great event. Humble as was His birth-place, a new star rested above the stable; and divine worship, offered by the manger where He lay, gave dignity to the lowly scene. His hands were rough with labour; but

at their touch eyes received their sight, and the dead were restored to life. His voice had been heard in the wails of infancy, and also in dying groans; but it quelled the roaring storm, and burst the ancient fetters of the tomb. His eye was quenched in darkness, fixed and filmy as He hung on the tree; but it had read the secrets of man's heart, and penetrated the veil of futurity. He did not walk the world in costly robes, or in imperial purple; but the hem of his garment, at the touch of faith, cured inveterate disease. He did not tread on luxurious carpets; but His step was on the billows of the sea. Unaccustomed to luxuries, His simple drink was water from the well; but water changed to wine at His bidding. No lordly halls received, or sumptuous banquets entertained, His guests; but the few fishes and five barley loaves of the mountain-feast were sufficient, in His hands, to satisfy the wants of thousands, and leave, of fragments, twelve baskets over.

The glory that shone through many of the

most humiliating scenes of His life was still more apparent in its closing hours. Men had left nothing undone to heap shame on His dying head, and aggravate by disgrace the bitterness of death. To pour contempt on His kingly claims they crowned His brows with thorns; in mockery of His omniscience, when they had blindfolded, they buffeted Him—asking whose was the hand that struck Him; in ridicule of His omnipotence, when they had nailed Him to the cross, they challenged Him to leave it—crying, with gibes and insults, and a cruelty His dying face had no power to soften, 'If thou be the Son of God, come down!' 'He saved others; himself he cannot save.' Yet even in this dark hour, when He was sinking into death under a cloud of shame and ignominy, see how the Son of man was glorified! To the Pharisees who, as He approached Jerusalem amid a gleam of passing popularity, and attended by a mighty crowd that hailed Him as their King, had asked Him to silence the hosannas of the people, He had said, 'If these should hold their peace, the stones would immediately cry out.' No empty boast! By-and-by that multitude melted away like a snow-wreath—like a flock of sheep when, crouching to the spring, the lion, with a bound and roar, leaps into the fold, the disciples have fled; and, save a dying robber that confesses our Lord, all men hold their peace. But now events happen more wonderful than ancient story relates of a dumb son who had followed his father to battle. Seeing him struck down, lying on the ground with a sword pointed at his breast, they tell how, under the sudden impulse of affection and of alarm for his father's life, he burst the string that tied his tongue, and cried out in terror. So when at Jesus's death all men held their peace, dumb nature spake. The rocks, whose bosoms, less hard than man's, were rent, cried out on earth; the sun, veiling his face from a scene on which insensate men looked without emotion, cried out in heaven; the dead, disturbed in their graves by so great a crime, cried out from their open tombs; and the temple, with its veil, though touched by no mortal hands, rent in twain from top to bottom, added its solemn testimony to theirs; and dying amid these strange, impressive, and transcendent wonders, in that of His death the hour had come when the Son of man was glorified.

2. Christ's death afforded the fullest display of His mercy, grace, and truth.

Not that they had not been displayed before— as in the wilderness, through which the pillar, symbol of His presence, their grateful shade by day and their light by night, guided and guarded the wandering host—as by the sea, whose waves rushed foaming and thundering together at His word to engulf beneath their waters the pride and power of Egypt—as on that desert with its barren sands covered day by day, for forty years, with corn dropped from dewy skies—as beside that gray rock which poured streams from its flinty bosom—as on that awful mountain which flamed like a volcano at His touch, and, striking the boldest with awe, shook with His thunders and trembled beneath His feet. In these, and in many other events, the forefathers of those who rejected our Lord had been the witnesses of His glory. He was the God of Sinai—the Captain of the host—the Angel of the Covenant; and for ages they had read in the Bible, and celebrated in the songs of the sanctuary, the wonders He had done in the days of their fathers, and in the old times before them.

Yet not till, veiling His divine splendours, the Son of God appeared in the form of a man, and, giving Himself up to death, expired amid the agonies of a cross, were His love and mercy, His pity, His purpose and His power to save, fully disclosed. It was when Moses smote the rock that its hidden treasures were unsealed; and the people, pressing eagerly forward—sons bearing aged parents on their shoulders, and mothers infants in their happy arms—heard the sweetest music in its liquid murmurs, and drank life in its cold gushing stream. It was when the alabaster box was broken that its value became known, and its aroma, rising from the head and feet of Jesus, was diffused throughout all the house. It is when the clusters of the grape, borne with songs from the vineyard by bright and happy maidens, are crushed in the wine-press, and trodden under foot, that they yield the wine which, used for sacred and also common purposes, was said to 'make glad the heart both of God and man.' Nor were Christ's gracious attributes, His love to poor sinners and His power to save them, fully disclosed till His dying hour; till He entered the garden where, sinking under the load of a world's guilt, He cried, 'My soul is exceeding sorrowful, even unto death;' till He hung on that cross where He poured out His precious blood a sacrifice for sin—dying the just for the unjust.

Had Jesus never died, nor heaven, nor hell, nor earth had ever known how He loved: nor had we, unable to imagine the degree and extent of His divine compassion, been constrained to exclaim, 'O the height and depth, the breadth and length, of the love of God!—it passeth knowledge.' No exaggeration this! Allying us more closely to God than the angels are—since His Son took not on Him the nature of angels, but the nature of man—and making these heavenly spirits our ministering servants, this love is 'higher than heaven;' saving in us those more guilty than devils are—since the devils never once rejected the Son of God, nor turned a deaf ear to the voice of mercy—this love is 'deeper than hell;' and infinitely surpassing any earthly affection, the measure thereof is 'longer than the earth, and broader than the sea.'

The full and crowning expression of the love wherewith God loved us in that, while we were enemies, He gave up His Son to die for us, and wherewith also His Son loved us in being willing to be given, at Jesus' death the hour arrived when, completing the great work of atonement, He was most fully glorified. He had been despised and rejected of men: He had been called an impostor, a blasphemer, a glutton, and a winebibber; neglected of His own creatures, He had seen their doors shut in His face, and been left, when the fox sought his hole and the bird dropt into her nest, to find a bed on the cold ground; persecuted in His cradle, He had been persecuted to His grave. But now His sorrows are past, and His shame rolled away for ever. He dies, but as a conqueror—crowned with the rich spoils of victory; a victim, but a victor also—crushing the head of the serpent that had bit His heel, and in the penitent thief whom He bears aloft to heaven, giving us a proof of His pity for the guilty, and of His willingness and power to save even the chief of sinners.

3. By His death, our Lord conquered hell, and death, and the grave.

It was the curse of Canaan, the descendant and representative of Ham, that he should be the servant of servants; but it is the crowning glory of Jesus that He became the conqueror of conquerors: spoiling principalities and powers, like a victor returning from the wars with monarchs and princes and captains bound to his chariot, He made a show of them openly. For forty days the haughty Philistine came forth to challenge the armies of the living God; crying, as he stalked out into the intervening meadow, and shook his plumes and spear in triumph, 'I defy Israel! Give me a man that we may fight together!' And since the fall, when Satan worsted our first parents, and laid their honour in the dust, for forty long centuries he had proudly held the field. No man had proved a match for him. In Noah, and Abraham, and Moses, and David, the very chiefs and standard-bearers of God's host had fallen; before his power and devilish subtlety, one after another bit the dust: nor had any been delivered from his cruel hand, but as Israel, when God, making a way of escape for His people, opened the gates of the sea, and snatched them from the grasp of Egypt.

But now the hour has come when this proud adversary of God and man has his challenge accepted. David's Son is buckling for the fight; angels are gathered on the battlements of heaven to watch its fortunes, and see the issue; each advancing from his own ranks, the Prince of Light and the Prince of Darkness meet. Foiled at all points, met with his match now, and more than his match, Satan is baffled and borne back: and yet—for such was the divine decree, the claims of justice, the price of victory—our Champion falls; but falls like Samson. He bows Himself on the pillars of His adversary's kingdom—by His own death destroying Death, and him that had the power of death, that is, the Devil. The Devil!— he had seduced angels from their loyalty, and had raised the shout of victory within the gates of Eden. Death!—he had plucked the crown from the brows of kings, and darkened the eyes of seers, and sealed the lips of prophets, and mocked the skill of man, and crushed the strength of giants: and, as Solomon says, in the war with him, men had found 'no discharge.' But how do the fortunes of battle change when Christ, our champion, the Captain of our salvation, comes into the field! Calling out, 'O death, I will be thy plagues! O grave, I will be thy destruction!' He takes the prey from the spoiler; and not only in our souls, washed in His blood and sanctified by His Spirit, redeems the jewel, but the casket too—for that purpose descending into the realms of the grave, with garments rolled in blood. The brow that bled beneath a crown of thorns now wears the diadem of victory; and now, where the eyes of men saw but a ghastly spectacle, a mangled body suspended on a tree, with the setting sun lighting up its dead, defaced, and pallid countenance, faith beholds the triumph of redeeming love—the crowning work and glory of the Son of God; and pointing to that sacred form which has death and the serpent lying crushed beneath its feet, she addresses men and angels, saying, 'Sing unto the Lord, for he hath triumphed gloriously: thy right hand, O Lord, hath dashed the enemy in pieces.'

The work of our Saviour was essentially and

pre-eminently that of a surety or substitute. Some affirm that Jesus died merely as an example, to teach us how to die. Others, repudiating the proper idea of an atonement, and emasculating a doctrine which they profess to hold, regard his death as nothing more than an expression of the love of God to a fallen world. But unless our blessed Lord assumed our nature that He might, besides fulfilling the requirements of the law, bear in some proper sense, and in our room and stead, the punishment due to sin, by what rule are we to interpret the language of Scripture? Were it otherwise, what language more misleading, more calculated to mislead, than these declarations?—'I am the good shepherd; the good shepherd giveth his life for the sheep; I lay down my life for the sheep'—'God commendeth his love toward us, in that, while we were yet sinners, Christ died for us'—'If, when we were enemies, we were reconciled to God by the death of his Son, much more being reconciled, we shall be saved by his life'—'Surely he hath borne our griefs, and carried our sorrows; he was wounded for our transgressions, he was bruised for our iniquities; the chastisement of our peace was upon him, and with his stripes we are healed.'

As is plain from these words, Jesus had to endure in our stead the penalty due to sin, and die for us, as the bleeding victim of old for him who offered it on the altar. Therefore it was, that they who knew not what they did when they crucified the Lord of glory, knew not what they said when they cast this cruel taunt in his face, 'He saved others, himself he cannot save!' This was true; but not for the reason they supposed. He could have saved Himself—descending from the cross to take summary vengeance on His foes; or as Samson did with the ponderous gates of Gaza, carry it away—rise before their astonished eyes, and bear it to heaven as a trophy of His power. What then? Alas! we had been left to perish.

The case may be in some measure illustrated by what happened in the terrible dilemma in which two miners once found themselves. They were engaged blasting a rock in the bowels of the earth. The chamber for the powder bored, they charge it; and having lighted the hissing match, they take to flight, hurrying to the bottom of the shaft, to throw themselves into the basket, and give the signal to be drawn up out of reach, not of danger only, but of death. Alas, the wheel turns not. The man at the top of the shaft is able to raise one, but not both. Every moment the fire may reach the powder, and blow them into eternity. There they sit; pale, speechless, helpless, looking each other in the face; and death staring grimly at them both. Both must die, unless one, sacrificing himself to save his comrade, leap from the basket. It was done—promptly, nobly done. They were, and yet were not, in equal danger. One is a man of God; the other a graceless, prayerless profligate. Calmly addressing his wicked companion, 'I know,' said the first, 'if you die, you go to hell; but knowing in whom I have believed, death shall be gain to me.' So bidding the other farewell, a Christian hero, he leaps from the basket; and leaving it to rise, sits down to pray and die. Here, though I may remark that this man himself escaped death by a singular providence, he saved the other, but himself also he could not save; and as there was there a physical impossibility of saving both, there is here a moral one. The justice of God which awarded the penalty of death to sin must be satisfied: the law of God which required perfect obedience must be magnified: the substitute or the sinner therefore must die; and Jesus died, the just for the unjust, that we might be saved—that whosoever believeth on Him might not perish, but have everlasting life.

The object of our faith, to whose righteousness, rejecting all confidence in our own, we trust, Jesus is also to be the object of our imitation—our pattern as well as our propitiation. Therefore they that are Christ's live not *to*, any more than they live *through*, themselves; the rule of their life, the motto blazoned on their banner, not self-indulgence, but self-denial. The spectators who, drawn to roof and window by the roar and tumult, looked down on the passing crowd as it hurried on to Calvary, knew Jesus by the cross on His shoulder, and the thorns on His bleeding brow. One eagerly pointing Him out to another—some with scorn on their lips, others with a tear in their eye—Yon is He, they cried, who looks so meek, and patient, and gentle, with a cross on his back and a crown of thorns on his brow! And still we may know the servant by the Master's livery. Who is mocked by an ungodly world? who blesses them that curse Him? who returns good for evil? who is patient with the bad? who toils and labours, spends and is spent, lives and perhaps dies for others, forgetful of himself? By the tokens whereby they recognized the Master, I recognize the man. If we can sit at ease while others are perishing around us—if we can lie on a flowery bank, basking in the gladsome sunshine, without taking any interest in others, or stretching out a hand to pluck them from the torrent that sweeps them on to ruin, it matters not to what church we belong. We belong not to Christ—we are none of His. As much as to murderers, adulterers, drunkards, and thieves, 'Depart from me, I have never known you,' is the language He shall hold to all whose life-maxim is expressed in such words as these, 'Am I my brother's keeper?'—let souls perish, so I be rich—let others suffer, so I enjoy myself—'Soul, take thine ease, eat, drink, and be merry.' Unless the same mind be in you that was in Jesus Christ, ye are none of His. Paul said, 'Christ liveth in me'—language which His humblest, weakest follower can hold as well as that great apostle. The beautiful incarnation of all that was lofty in aim, tender in sympathy, generous in heart, pure in life, self-forgetful, and self-denying, Jesus Himself is the fair copy which Christians, through the aids of the Holy Spirit, are to attempt to imitate. 'If any man,' He said, 'would be my disciple, let him take up his cross, deny himself daily, and follow me.'

VIII.

THE WAY OF SALVATION.

SOME Scripture terms are forensic. Such are the expressions *justified* and *condemned*. Employed in courts of law, they call up to our minds the scene of a trial—the crowd of eager spectators; the prisoner standing alone, pale and anxious, at the bar; the judges seated aloft in imposing state; the heavy indictment; the long array of witnesses; the sudden and breathless silence, amid which—all bending forward to catch their words—the jury return into court with their verdict; the verdict itself, the Not Guilty or Guilty, that sends the accused away to life and liberty, or, falling from reluctant lips, and going like a knife to his heart, sends him to the scaffold and seals his doom. The expressions 'justified' and 'condemned,' therefore, forewarn us of a day when, with God for his judge, an assembled world for spectators, and heaven or hell for his destiny, every man shall be put upon his trial; judged according to the deeds done in the body, whether they were good or evil. 'It is appointed,' says an Apostle, 'unto men once to die, but after this the judgment.'

A solemn, but a certain prospect!—for none may hope to escape this ordeal. Universal as the sentence, judgment is inevitable as the scythe of death. It is often wonderful to see how human justice tracks the steps and doublings of a guilty fugitive, like a sleuth-hound; and how, with an arm that stretches over broad continents and seas, she will drag him to her bar from his hiding-place in the ends of the earth. Yet, cases ever and anon occur where the gallows, if I may use the expression, is cheated of its due, and the perpetrators of crimes that have struck society with horror escape detection, or elude the keenest pursuit. But escape from God and His judgment is impossible. Reconciled to Him through the blood of His Son, and recognizing their Saviour in the Judge before whose face—as He comes with ten times ten thousand angels—the heavens flee away, God's people would not escape though they could; and as to His enemies, who vainly cry on the mountains and rocks to cover them, they could not though they would. What says one who may be supposed, under a sense of guilt and dread of punishment, to have been racking his fancy for a way to elude the presence and escape the justice of God? 'Whither,' he asks, 'shall I go from thy Spirit? Whither shall I flee from thy presence? If I ascend up to heaven, thou art there; if I make my bed in hell, behold, thou art also there; if I take the wings of the morning, and dwell in the uttermost parts of the sea, there shall thy hand lead me; if I say, Surely the darkness shall cover me, even the night shall be light about me.' Nor do God's own words, any more than these, leave a chance, the shadow of a hope, the smallest loophole of escape, to impenitent and unbelieving sinners. To alarm them, to persuade them to abandon their sins and embrace the Saviour, He uses the boldest figures. Speaking of the wicked, He says, 'He that fleeth of them shall not flee away; and he that escapeth of them shall not be delivered; though they dig into hell, there shall mine hand take them; though they climb up to heaven, there will I bring them down; though they be hid from my sight in the bottom of the sea, there will I command the serpent, and he shall bite them.'

Another great difference between the administration of Divine and human justice, lies in this, that while none shall escape God's judgment, its sentence, once passed, whether for good or evil, is irrevocable. A very weighty and solemn consideration! As the tree falls, so it lies; they that are filthy shall be filthy still, as they that are righteous shall be righteous still. At an earthly tribunal hope sustains the criminal, when, pity taking the place of horror, every eye regards him with sorrow, and the voice of the judge trembles with emotion, as, amid an awful silence, he pronounces the words of doom. What though the 'condemned cell' receives him now? He reads above its gloomy door no such words as Dante has inscribed on the gates of hell, 'Let them who enter here leave Hope behind!' Abandon the wretch who may, hope does not; but goes with him from the bar, shining into his heart like the sunbeam that falls through his grated window on the floor. In other cases justice has relented somewhat of her sternness. Why may she not in his? So, down to the last post, and the last day, and the last hour, clinging to hope as a drowning man to a plank, many whom earthly tribunals have consigned to death, have illustrated and verified the saying—

> 'As long as life its term extends,
> Hope's blest dominion never ends.'

But despair, more terrible than the devils old painters represent dragging away the lost, seizes those whom God condemns—let me say, condemns reluctant. He is not willing that any should perish; He 'so loved the world that he gave up his only-begotten Son, that whosoever believeth in him might not perish, but have everlasting life;' yet, the great white throne once set, the books once opened, the sentence once passed, 'He hath forgotten to be gracious, and his mercy is clean gone for ever,' it is idle quarrelling with that truth: 'Shall not the Judge of all the earth do right?' and in our imperfect knowledge of the Infinite and of His ways, to challenge them is for the clay to say to the potter, Why hast thou made me thus? It is certain that with salvation purchased at an enormous cost, and not only freely offered, but earnestly and affectionately pressed on the chief of sinners, we shall not have to blame God, but ourselves, if we are lost. It is not by God's hand, but our own—not from within, but from without, the door of heaven is barred. 'Ye will not come unto me,' says Jesus. Now, taking God's word as it stands, what is the plain, practical conclusion to which the irrevocable nature of the sentence leads, but this, that unlike such as are arraigned at man's bar, we are to apply for pardon, not after, but before our trial —before death has summoned, or the Judge has sentenced us. It is too late then. Then, in the words of the bridegroom to the foolish virgins, 'The door is shut!'

History relates the story of a man, a sagacious and far-sighted man, whose example it is our safety, our salvation to follow. He had committed heinous crimes against his sovereign and the state. He knew his life to be forfeited; and that if, allowing events to take their course, he waited to be tried, he was certain to be condemned. The case is exactly ours. In these circumstances he repaired to the palace to fling himself at the feet of his sovereign, and making full confession of his crimes, to beg for mercy. Through the clemency of his king, and the intercession of a powerful friend at court, he found mercy; and, with a full pardon in his bosom, signed by the king's own hand, left the royal presence a happy man. In course of time, the day of trial arrives, gathering a great concourse of people. He repairs to the place. Ignorant of his secret, anxious friends tremble for his fate; and the spectators wonder at his calm and placid bearing as he passes the scaffold where they think he is so soon to die, and enters the court, certain, as they fancy, to be condemned. He steps up to the bar as lightly as a bridegroom to the marriage altar; and, to all men's surprise, looks boldly around, on the court, his judges, and his accusers. At this, however, they cease to wonder when, after listening unmoved to charges enough to hang twenty men in place of one, he thrusts his hand into his bosom to draw forth the pardon, to cast it on the table, and find himself, amid a sudden outburst of joy, locked in the happy embraces of his wife and children. Let us go and do likewise. The bar of Divine judgment is a place not to sue for mercy, but to plead it. Appearing there robed in the righteousness of Jesus Christ, justified, forgiven, in our hands a pardon signed and sealed with blood, we shall look around us undismayed on all the terrors of the scene—to ask with Paul, 'Who shall lay anything to the charge of God's elect? It is God that justifieth; who is he that condemneth?'

I remark that the way of salvation lies in being justified, not through our own, but imputed righteousness.

'All we like sheep have gone astray'—'The Scripture hath concluded all under sin'—'By the offence of one, judgment came upon all men unto condemnation'—'Death passed upon all men, for that all have sinned'—'Cursed is every one that continueth not in all things written in the book of the law to do them'—these, the words of Scripture, sound like the clank of fetters. In the face of such declarations, what folly is it in a man to attempt to beguile his conscience; to quiet its fears; persuading himself that, safe in the mercy from the justice of God, he has no need to be alarmed at the prospect of death and judgment! Would that these words spoke as pointedly to our hearts as they speak plainly to our ears! Guilt has been incurred; there is a judgment to come, and a pressing necessity, if there be a way of escape, that we should take it; take it now; take it at whatever cost—as our Lord says, plucking out a right eye, and cutting off a right hand, and losing our life that we may find it.

There is such a way; but certainly not by the works of the law. In perfect harmony with Him who pronounces our 'righteousnesses to be filthy rags,' Paul says, 'By the deeds of the law shall no flesh be justified;' and in that sets up such a notice as turns one back from a road where, though once frequented, the grass, growing rank and tall, has obliterated every footmark. Ever since the Fall, the gate to heaven by the law has stood shut, nor once turned on its hinges; the rust of long ages there, and over it a notice— 'No passage this way.' Yet, blessed be God, there is a way of return to His favour, forgiveness, and the kingdom of heaven. Harlots, publicans, and sinners have found it; and why may not we? To make it, God's Son became a man, taking to Himself a body that He might be capable of suffering;—eyes to weep; a brow to bleed beneath the thorns; feet and hands, that, with the iron driven through the quivering flesh, He might hang, a sacrifice for sin, on the accursed tree. He was made under the law for the very purpose of answering its demands, both in the way of doing and of suffering. He became a man for the very purpose of being a man of sorrows; and shared in our nature for the very purpose of suffering in our stead. There is a story of a brave sacrifice once made to save the life of a king. The battle had gone against him. Separated by accident from his followers, he was hard bested; a swarm of foes pressed on him—their swords ringing on his helmet, and each eager to obtain the honours that were to reward his capture or death. He dies unless some one will die in his room. A chivalrous follower sees the peril; spurs his horse into the thick of the foe, shouting, as he whirled his bloody battle-blade above his head, 'I am the king!' and thus turned against his own bosom the swords that had otherwise been buried in his master's. A generous, heroic sacrifice! yet but a faint shadow of what He offered who laid down His life a ransom, not for His friends, but His enemies; dying, the just for the unjust, that we might be saved.

Distinguished in death as in His life and divine nature from all other men, our Lord Jesus Christ, in dying, did not pay the debt of nature, or, as it may be properly called, the debt of sin, for Himself. He did not die because He was a sinner, but a substitute; because He was a debtor, but a surety—all the sufferings borne by Him from His cradle to the grave being ours, the payment of debts incurred by us and undertaken by Him. Fulfilling all the precepts it enjoined, and paying all the penalties it required, He rendered a perfect obedience to the Divine law. This constitutes His righteousness, or merits; and since God is pleased to accept that in lack and place of ours, there can be no condemnation for those who, rejecting all confidence in their own righteousness to trust in His, are in Jesus Christ, and prove themselves to be so by walking, not after the flesh, but after the Spirit.

How there not only *is*, but *can be* no condemnation for them, I may illustrate by the case of two Greeks whom friendship had bound in the most endearing ties. One, condemned to die for some offence, wishes, ere he leaves the world, to go away that he may arrange his affairs, and see his family, and bid them a last farewell. In these circumstances, and with a love deserving such a garland as David, saying, 'Very pleasant hast thou been unto me, my brother Jonathan; thy love to me was wonderful, passing the love of women,' laid on the grave of Jonathan—his friend undertook, in case he did not return, to suffer death in his stead. The offer was accepted; and was nearly attended with a tragic result.

The day of doom arrives, but not the criminal. Nor was it till the very hour arrived, and the procession, with his surety ready to die, had reached the scaffold, that he, detained at sea by adverse winds, appears; shouts to them from afar to stay the execution; and forcing his way through the crowd, leaps on the scaffold to push aside his substitute, and, like a brave, true man, bare his own neck to the sword. Touched by the display of such tender and rare affection—the joy of the one that he was in time to save his surety, the grief of the other that he had lost the opportunity of dying for his friend—the people, yielding to a generous impulse, and in honour of such noble friendship, decreed that neither should perish. But suppose that things had fallen out otherwise, and that the substitute had suffered the penalty of the law before the true criminal had time to reach the scene, and arrest the stroke. What then? Why, then the law had nothing to say to him. Though guilty, he was free; and, as he looked with weeping eyes on the pale face and dead body of his generous friend, he could raise his head to look around on spectators, officers, and executioner, saying, 'Who shall lay anything to my charge?' Nor had his prayer been granted though, unwilling to survive his friend and prolong a life that had lost its relish, he had implored death at their hands. Since his surety had paid the penalty, the justice that demanded his death before would refuse it now. The demands of the law had been satisfied; and had an angry crowd, suspecting that he had wilfully delayed his return, attempted violence against his person, the very sword that had been buried in the bosom of the substitute had been drawn in defence of his. The death of innocence had saved the life of guilt.

Now as, on such a supposition, it had happened in that case, it does happen in the case of all who, through faith in our surety, the Lord Jesus Christ, receive the righteousness that makes the sinner just. His perfect merits imputed to them—His work and sufferings accounted theirs

—the justice that demanded their condemnation once demands their acquittal now; the law, with all its requirements, now fully satisfied, is no longer against, but for them; all God's attributes are on their side now; and so, instead of fleeing from justice, like Adam when he fled for shelter to the bush, they claim protection now from their enemies—Satan, and hell, and fear, and guilt—as much from Jehovah's justice as from Jehovah's mercy. No creditor can righteously demand that a debt be twice paid; nor magistrate that a crime be twice punished; nor sovereign that a tax be twice exacted. And 'shall man be more just than God?' Is that justice on the part of man? and 'Are not my ways equal?' saith the Lord. Jesus has once for all paid the debt of His people to the uttermost farthing; fulfilled their duties, and made full atonement for their crimes. And hence their joy and peace in believing; hence the happy confidence with which, like the dying Wesley, when his spirit was hovering on the verge of another world, they who have made their calling and election sure, can sing—

> 'I the chief of sinners am;
> But Jesus died for me.'

Regarding the method of salvation by faith in the righteousness of Jesus Christ as a way, here are some of its peculiar and gracious and happy features, borrowed from the lights of prophecy.

It is a *high way*.

A highway, or the 'King's highway,' as it used to be called, is distinguished from private roads by an important difference. Gates, walls, and warnings may exclude from these all but members or visitors of the family to whose mansions they lead; but this is free to the public— the whole public. Here, no man challenges my right to walk, or, holding the gate in hand, and saying 'Back, back,' compels me with wearied feet and disappointed hopes to retrace my steps. Here, no distinctions of noble or mean, of rich or poor, of virtuous or vicious, of good or bad, of sect, or rank, or party, are recognized. Here all classes—master and servant, the peer in his robes and the beggar in his rags—meet on common ground; the road below as free to every foot as the air above to birds of every wing.

Nor less free is salvation by faith in Jesus Christ. Not that men, encroaching as well on the prerogatives of the Sovereign as on the rights and privileges of His people, have not wickedly attempted to restrict the blessings of grace. For example—denying the free use of the Scriptures to the laity, claiming for her priests a monopoly of spiritual power, and, for her adherents, the exclusive benefits of the kingdom of heaven, this Popery does. And other churches, retaining her spirit, though they repudiate her name, show themselves hardly less exclusive. Some confining the flow of grace to the channel of what they call 'Apostolical Succession;' others regarding their own as the only true and faithful church, without whose pale, often of the narrowest limits, there is little hope of a blessing either on sermons or sacraments, take from salvation by faith in

Christ's righteousness the characteristic features of a highway. But in the face of invitations so free as these,—' Ho every one that thirsteth, come ye to the waters,'—' Come unto me, all ye that labour and are heavy laden, and I will give you rest,'—in the face also of declarations so gracious as these,—' Whosoever cometh unto me I will in no wise cast out,'—' Whosoever believeth in me shall not perish, but hath everlasting life,' —it is bold, and nothing less than impious presumption to attempt to dam up the living waters of the sanctuary, and confine to the narrow limits of their own sect or party the benefits of Christ's death. God be praised, they cannot. They may as well prescribe a narrower course for the great sun as he goes forth in the heavens to shine on every land; or control the tides, that, rising to celestial influences, roll over the bosom of the ocean to visit every continent and wash every shore. Inviting all, without respect to birth or baptism, to character or church, addressing as much the vilest sinners, the outcasts, the scum and dregs of society, as those whose virtues have won universal esteem, Jesus says, 'Look unto me and be ye saved, all ye ends of the earth'—'I am the way'—'I have set before you an open door.' And neither deterred by the voice of bigotry nor scared by the fears of guilt, let us crowd the gates of mercy; enter—enter joyfully in. Blessed be God, He who shutteth and no man openeth, openeth and no man shutteth.

It is a *plain way.*

The Bible has had innumerable commentators. Some, by their books or sermons, remind us of him who lighted a candle to show the sun; and others, like the fog-bank through which the sun shines shorn of his beams, 'darken counsel by words,' and make what was clear obscure. By their labours, some have diluted, while others, making their sermons or commentaries a vehicle for error, have adulterated the truth of God, the wine of life. But however this may be, more pens have been worn, more breath spent, more printing-presses employed, in explaining the Bible than all other books whatever; so that were all the books collected which have been written to throw light on the Scriptures, they would—not excepting that of Alexandria, which it took many weeks to reduce to ashes—form the largest library the world ever saw. Are we to infer from this that the way of life is obscure? By no means. All that it is necessary to know in order to be saved, it is easy to know. 'The wayfaring men, though fools, shall not err therein,' says the Prophet; and without disparaging the labours of pious and able divines to explore the mysteries and shed light on the obscurities of the sacred volume, the simple Bible, blessed by God, has proved to unlettered thousands a safe and sufficient guide. Whatever genius and arduous study it may require to rise to a place in the temple of fame, many a humble Christian, hardly able to spell his way through the Word of God, has reached one in the temple of heaven. Thousands so deficient in talent or energy as never to have been able to make their way in this world, have found their way to a better one; nor are there wanting interesting and well-attested cases of imbeciles, who, though destitute of capacity for ordinary knowledge, have known Him whom to know is life eternal—so plain the way through child-like faith in Christ—so easy as well to the unsteady gait of simpletons as to the tottering foot of childhood, as to verify the words, 'The wayfaring men, though fools, shall not err therein.' With this simple answer to the great question, 'What shall I do to be saved?' 'Believe on the Lord Jesus Christ, and thou shalt be saved,' none need be excluded from heaven because of ignorance; as with virtue in Christ's blood to cleanse the chief of sinners, none need be excluded because of sin. It needs no learning to learn this way.

What has the Church seen? God ordaining strength out of the mouth of babes and sucklings; grey-haired men learning wisdom at the feet of childhood; the death-beds of the humble poor like the very gates of heaven; the child learning the way to life on a mother's knee; the thief learning it on his dying cross; the mantle of prophets falling on ploughmen; heaven revealing its glories to humble shepherds; rude fishermen of Galilee called to the apostleship; grace polishing the roughest men; roaming savages tamed by the voice and sitting at the feet of Jesus, clothed and in their right mind. Simple faith in Him is all that is required—such confidence as the little child, lying in its mother's arms, hanging on her neck, looking up in her face, reposes in the power of a mother's arm and the tenderness of a mother's heart.

It is a *holy way*.

> 'Just as I am, without one plea,
> But that Thy blood was shed for me,
> And that Thou bid'st me come to Thee,
> O Lamb of God, I come.'

As is expressed in these well-known and beautiful lines, we are to go to Christ as sinners—guilty, polluted, wretched, miserable sinners. We are to go as we are; not, however, to continue as we are, but to obtain deliverance as well from the power as from the punishment of sin. Regarding it as a disease, hereditary in our family, deadly as the leprosy, and as loathsome in its features as it is fatal in its issue, the Church may be regarded as an hospital—but by no means an hospital for incurables. To those asylums where pity seeks to shelter the hopeless and alleviate the sufferings of lingering but inevitable death, the gospel presents no counterpart. With a physician in Christ, of whom I can say that He never refused a case, never charged a fee, and never lost a patient, it opens its doors to receive the sick, men and women, even in the very hour and article of death; but it is to cure them—send them out healed; through the sanative and sanctifying influence of the Holy Spirit, cured of 'whatsoever manner of disease they had.'

Neither requiring nor recognizing any merit in us, but resting our acceptance with God entirely on the merits of His Son, the gospel does not dispense with personal holiness, nor afford any pretext to such as say, Let us continue in sin, that grace may abound. The same authority that declares, Whosoever believeth on the Lord Jesus Christ shall be saved, declares that without holiness no man shall see God. A prominent feature that, of salvation by faith in the righteousness of Jesus Christ—' it shall be called,' says the prophet, ' the way of holiness: the unclean shall not pass over it.' In regeneration, this way is entered on by a holy change; in the saints of God, it is frequented by a holy company; and in that pure and blessed heaven, above whose portals is written, There entereth nothing here to hurt or to defile, it conducts to a holy place.

Where are you going? said Malan, of Geneva, to an English lady who was introduced to him. I am on my way to visit Rome, was her reply. Oh, he answered, that is not what I mean; startling her with this plain, pointed question, Is it to heaven or to hell, madam, you are going? Abrupt, indiscreet perhaps, as such a mode of address may be considered, the question is one which every person should put to themselves—proving their own work, trying the foundation of their hopes, and giving all diligence, as the Apostle says, to make their calling and election sure. For this object, what better, plainer, surer test than the holiness which the Scriptures invariably associate with true living faith? There sanctification and justification are inseparably connected; and what God hath joined together, let none attempt to put asunder. To live in the unrestrained, unrepented indulgence of any sin, and talk of faith in Christ, and indulge in hopes of heaven, is a mockery and a miserable delusion; one of the strongest proofs that 'the heart is deceitful above all things, and desperately wicked.' To be holy as God is holy, to be perfect as our Father in heaven is perfect, to have the same mind in us that was in Jesus Christ, though not yet the attainment, is the aim and wish, the object of the prayers and efforts, of every child of God—No holiness, no heaven, being an adage as true as the more common saying, No cross, no crown.

It is a *safe way*.

'He laid his carcase in his own grave, and they mourned over him, saying, Alas, my brother!' That grave received one who was returning to a home he never reached. Contrary to his instructions, this prophet of God had ate and drunk in Bethel to learn, that when he left the path of duty, he left the path of safety. On his way homeward, a lion, the messenger of divine wrath, met and slew him. This was no accident, but a special providence—as appeared from the circumstance that the beast which he rode was found standing fearless on one side of his body, and the lion that had killed him quietly on the other; yet such accidents were not uncommon in the lands of the Bible. Jacob, for instance, when the coat of many colours was produced, all stained with blood, instantly and bitterly exclaimed, It is my son's coat, an evil beast hath devoured him; Joseph, without doubt, is rent in pieces. So also David, describing the greatness of his danger, says, 'My soul is among lions;' and hence, also, the figure employed to describe the difficulty or peril of an enterprise, 'There is a lion in the path!'

Blessed be God, this cannot be said of the path opened to heaven by the blood of Christ. 'No lion shall be there,' says the prophet, 'nor any ravenous beast shall go up therein; it shall not be found there'—words these that, describing the state of those who are justified through faith in the righteousness of Jesus Christ, assure us of their safety, of the care the Lord takes of them; preserving them; defending them; and securing this, that come what may in the form of trials and temptations, they shall not come short of eternal life. Were it otherwise, what though salvation were freely offered, and offered to all, if any honestly seeking and pursuing it might nevertheless perish! What though Christ died, if any for whom He died could be plucked out of His hands! Farewell then to the peace that passeth understanding; farewell to the calm tranquillity that is careful for nothing, but by prayer and supplication, with thanksgiving in all things, makes its wants known unto God. It is with cautious steps we tread the grass where the serpent lies coiled, ready for the spring; it is with beating heart, and anxious eye, and hushed and breathless silence, travellers skirt the brake where the lion, watching for his prey, lies crouching for the leap; and, if exposed without protection to such dangers, how is the pilgrim to Zion to go up with songs? how is he to respond to the glorious call, Rejoice in the Lord alway, and again I say, Rejoice?

'Let not your heart be troubled,' said Jesus; 'ye believe in God, believe also in me.' So He says to His people; and what says He of them?—'I give unto them eternal life, and they shall never perish.' There were lions once in the way. Satan was one—a roaring lion walking about seeking whom he might devour: but he is chained now, and able to do little more than roar against the saints; he may alarm, but cannot harm them. The justice of God also was once a lion in the way: but the Good Shepherd having given His life for the sheep, justice has been satisfied, and now the lion and the lamb dwell together. Death also was once a lion in the way; but sin, the sting of death, atoned for, he has lost his terrors; direst foe is changed into truest friend; death has become gain, and in its darkness faith hails the aurora of eternal day. No doubt, they who are united by faith to Christ, accepted and forgiven of God, have evils to endure in this life; a sore battle to fight; perhaps heavy burdens to bear. But though they may be cast down, they cannot be destroyed. With Jesus at the helm, their ship may be tossed on the billows, but it cannot founder. In reward of what He did and suffered for them, God hath promised to His Son what He promised to His servant, Paul, 'I have given thee all them that sail with thee!' so—as when the ship took the ground, and her masts went by the board, and the waves made a clean breach over her, some swimming, some on boards, some drifting through the wild sea on broken pieces of the ship, all that company escaped safe to land, all who believe in Jesus shall reach the heavenly shore. I say, therefore, with Paul, Wherefore, sirs, be of good cheer!

> 'Through Him all dangers we'll defy,
> And more than conquer all.'

IX.

THE SINNER'S LINK TO THE SAVIOUR—FAITH.

EVERY candid reader of the Bible is struck with the singular prominence which it gives to Faith. It is obvious at a glance that Faith is the pivot on which the whole system of divine truth turns. It is so, alike in theory and in practice; theoretically, as the corner-stone of the system of doctrine; and practically, as the foundation of the new life of the Christian. It is said that we are justified by faith, and being so justified, we have peace with God through Jesus Christ our Lord. By faith also we have access into a state of abiding grace, and rejoice in the hope of the glory of God. Without faith, we are told, it is impossible to please God. Faith was the one great attribute of all the Old Testament saints, even of men who differed from one another so widely as Enoch differed from Samson, or as Isaac differed from Jephthah. By faith the elders obtained a good report; it was alike the support of their hopes, the fountain of their courage, the source of their patience, and the instrument of their victories. From our Lord nothing drew so cordial commendations as the victories of faith; of the centurion he could say, 'I have not found so great faith, no, not in Israel;' and to the Syrophenician mother, 'O woman, great is thy faith; be it unto thee even as thou wilt.' In the Acts of the Apostles the highest praise bestowed on martyrs and heroes rests upon the glory of their faith; Stephen was full of faith and power, so that his face shone as it had been the face of an angel; Barnabas was a good man, full of the Holy Ghost and of faith; and Paul describes his new life in Christ as very eminently a life of faith: 'The life that I live in the flesh, I live by the faith of the Son of God, who loved me and gave himself for me.'

In any attempt, then, to set forth the leading truths of Christianity a prominent place is due to faith. What does it really mean? How comes it to fulfil a function so important as that which is assigned to it in the word of God? How comes it to be the link that binds the sinner to the Saviour, the hand that lays hold upon Christ, the medium by which all saving blessings come? How is it that faith is made the great criterion for determining the state of salvation, and that the most awful issues of life and death are suspended on its presence or absence? For 'He that believeth on the Son hath everlasting life; but he that believeth not the Son shall not see life; but the wrath of God abideth on him.' These are great questions, demanding the most earnest attention of all who would attain to the knowledge of saving truth.

1. We begin by explaining the term. In the most general sense of the word, faith denotes the

act or state of mind which receives as true any statement made on the authority or by the lips of God. This is quite obvious in reference to the faith brought under our notice in the Old Testament. Thus, it was communicated to Abraham on the authority of God that he was to have a son, and that through that son his posterity would be like the stars of heaven; Abraham believed the communication, even though in the circumstances there was no human probability or even possibility of its fulfilment. It was further communicated to Abraham, on God's authority, that through this son, or through the seed that should spring from him, all the families of the earth should be blessed; and so strong was Abraham's belief in this, that even when he was called to offer up that child of promise in sacrifice, he rested in the conviction that rather than let the promise fail, God would raise him up, even from the dead. It will be seen, on a moment's reflection, that the nature of the act of faith was somewhat different in reference to these two things. In the former, what

Abraham was called to believe, was simply a historical fact,—the fact, namely, that he was to be the progenitor of a great posterity; no doubt a gratifying fact for him, but not directly affecting his personal state before God, nor his welfare for the life to come. But in the second instance, more was demanded of him than the simple belief of a historical fact. The communication from God, that in his seed all the nations of the earth would be blessed, included himself as well as others, himself as a sinner, guilty before God, and needing a Saviour. This communication was something for him to rest on, and to derive hope and comfort from, whenever the sense of sin should weigh heavily on his conscience, or the sense of a needed righteousness, better than his own, should fill him with anxiety. Thus there was more of the spirit of *trust* in this exercise of faith than in the other. The promise of God here was something for Abraham to lean on, to calm his fears and inspire his hopes when evil seemed to be pressing in on him and on the world, when the sky was darkening and sounds of a gathering tempest falling upon his ears.

Hence it appears that when faith in God's word is real, it will affect the person believing it differently according to the nature of the thing believed, and according to the relation to it of the person believing. If it be a matter intimately affecting his dearest interests, his whole soul will be set in motion by it; if it be a matter with which he has only a distant connection, hardly an emotion will be stirred.

We see what is analogous to this in the intercourse of man with man. You tell a man that some bank, in which all his property is invested, has suddenly failed—a horror of great darkness comes over him. You tell the same thing to some one who has no interest in the matter— hardly a line in his face is changed. You tell a poor man that a rich neighbour is dead—he is grieved and alarmed, for he has been supported by his bounty. You tell the same thing to another—he can hardly suppress his joy, for he is heir to his fortune.

So, also, when any statement made on God's authority is really believed. If it is felt to imply evil, it will excite fear; if it is felt to imply good, it will excite joy. It is quite possible that a statement implying evil may excite no fear, or a statement implying good may excite no joy. But in such cases, there cannot be real faith. There was no real faith on the part of Eve when she ate the apple—the devil's lie was what she believed in in preference and in opposition to the truth of God. But there was real faith on the part of Noah, when, *moved with fear*, he prepared an ark to the saving of his house. There was real faith on the part of the Ninevites when, hearing Jonah's message, they humbled themselves before God. There was real faith on the part of David, when he heard from Nathan that the great Deliverer was to be born of his seed, and his whole heart went out in thanksgivings. There was real faith on the part of Mary, when the angel announced that she was to give birth to the Messiah,—no higher joy was ever felt than hers, 'My soul doth magnify the Lord, and my spirit doth rejoice in God my Saviour.'

In those instances in which the statement believed referred to a Person by whom certain blessings were to come, the belief that resulted had in it the nature of *trust*. Thus it was when God called on the oppressed Israelites to receive Moses as their Deliverer. He announced His purpose of achieving their deliverance through him; He gave them to understand that His Spirit would be poured out on him as a spirit of wisdom, of power, and of authority; in short, that nothing would be wanting to constitute him a triumphant champion. Evidently, where there was faith in these promises, there would be trust in Moses. The people would lean confidently on him as fully qualified to deliver, and in consequence they would have a thorough sense of safety, whatever difficulties or opposition might arise. And the more they showed of this spirit of trust when the circumstances were adverse, so much the more highly would they honour God. If dangers multiplied around them, dangers that threw their unbelieving brethren into despair; by remaining calm and confident they would show that, whatever might be the appearances, there was no real cause for anxiety. God, they would say, is our refuge, and Moses is His servant, therefore we will not fear—all must be well.

2. These simple explanations bear on faith generally; we go on to remark that the faith with which eternal life is specially connected in the New Testament, bears upon the statements which God has made about our salvation through Jesus Christ.

These statements are of a two-fold character: the one respecting the evil that has been incurred; the other respecting the good that has been provided.

Regarding the evil that has been incurred, God's statements are very terrible. All sin, in God's eyes, is a frightful crime and deserves a frightful punishment. Men may have such want of moral sensibility as not to understand why this should be, they may be unable to detect in sin that character of vileness which makes it so detestable to God, and its doom so awful. Be this as it may, there is no doubt as to the view of sin which the Scriptures attribute to God — 'The wrath of God is revealed from heaven against all ungodliness and unrighteousness of men who hold the truth in unrighteousness.' The commonness of sin, which takes so much away from its odious character in our eyes, makes no difference to it in God's. Though it be the universal characteristic of our race; though all have sinned and come short of the glory of God; though its corrupting stain has spread to every part of our nature; though it meets the eye of the Holy One alike in the crowded city and in the lonely cottage, on the throne of the Prince and under the rags of the beggar, it never ceases to present to Him the same horrid aspect—the abominable thing which He hates; and so long as filth is hateful to purity, so long as light can have no fellowship with darkness, the doom of sin and of the sinner must remain unchangeable—'The soul that sinneth, it shall die.'

On the other hand, God's statements to us regarding the good that has been provided in Christ, are equally striking. 'The wages of sin is death; but the gift of God is eternal life, through Jesus Christ our Lord.' 'Christ hath redeemed us from the curse of the law, being made a curse for us.' 'Christ hath also once suffered for sin, the just for the unjust, that he might bring us unto God.' The remedy for sin is complete, altogether satisfactory to God, and the offer of the remedy is as wide as the globe and as free as the air. 'Ho, every one that thirsteth, come ye to the waters, and he that hath no money.' 'Look unto me, and be ye saved, all ye ends of the earth; for I am God, and beside me there is none else.' 'Come unto me, all ye that labour and are heavy laden, and I will give you rest.' Redemption from sin, indeed, is the crowning product of divine skill and power; and wide and deep though the ruin be which sin has caused, the remedy of the Gospel is amply sufficient to counteract its curse, and restore the forfeited blessing; for 'where sin abounded, grace did much more abound; that as sin hath reigned unto death, even so might grace reign through righteousness unto eternal life, through Jesus Christ our Lord.'

Now, wherever faith is exercised in these two classes of statements, the reality of the faith will be seen by the fear which results from believing the one, and the joy which accompanies the reception of the other. On the day of Pentecost, first the one class of statements and then the other were successively brought to bear on the thousands that hung on the lips of Peter. When they believed the statement of evil incurred, they were pricked in their heart, and driven to the borders of despair; when they heard of the good provided, they 'gladly' received the word, their hearts were filled with joy and peace. When the Philippian jailor believed the first, he cried out, what must I do to be saved? When he believed the second, he was baptized, believing in the Lord with all his house. It is obvious that the process of faith is fundamentally incomplete, unless both classes of statements are received with equal earnestness. Sometimes there is a great disproportion, the first class of statements are received, almost devoured, and the other hardly permitted to be entertained. And sometimes, on the other hand, but little regard is had to the first, and no hesitation is felt as to the second. Many persons have religion enough to make them fear, but not enough to make them rejoice. They stop short on the narrow isthmus that leads from fear to joy, like one driven from a burning house on a winter night, who stands shivering in the street and cannot be prevailed on to enter the open door of his neighbour. Miserable halting-place! opposed alike to the nature of man, and to the purpose of God. Man was never made to rest in a state of fear. Equilibrium in fear is as much an impossibility for the heart of man as equilibrium for a ship in the midst of a gale. And God never meant His intelligent creatures to abide in fear. If ever He bids them fear, it is that He may presently bid them fear not. It is 'fear not' that is the constant exhortation of the Bible. And why? Not because there is no occasion for fear, but because there is transcendant occasion for joy. Not because sin has brought no curse, but because Jesus has brought a transcendant blessing. Not because Paradise has never been lost, but because God, according to His abundant mercy, hath provided a better inheritance—'incorruptible, and undefiled, and that fadeth not away.'

On the other hand, there are persons who pay little attention to what is said of the evil incurred, and have no difficulty in receiving the tidings of redemption. Their sense of sin is slight, and their faith, if it be at all genuine, has but shallow roots. They are disposed to regard the moral difficulty caused by sin as no very serious one, and to rest in the thought that all has been easily and satisfactorily adjusted. We would not affirm that all such persons are destitute of true faith in God's statements regarding salvation. But we fear that, as a rule, the easy-going manner in which the whole subject is treated indicates a heart unmoved by the solemn message. We remember reading some years ago in a daily London newspaper, an apology for the prevalent gaiety of the population on Good Friday. With a jaunty nonchalance the writer remarked that the people might well be gay on the anniversary of a day that had removed all cause for gloom. A clever caricature of the Scripture doctrine! A kind of jumble of the two classes of statements, regarding man's guilt and God's grace, out of which an easy-going 'All's right,' seems to be the outcome! The experience of the day of Pentecost was something widely different. And very different is the experience of all who can say, 'O Lord, I will praise thee; though thou wast angry with me, thine anger is turned away, and thou comfortedst me.'

3. More explicitly we go on to remark that the statements of God regarding the salvation that has been provided relate mainly to the person and the work of Christ, and therefore the faith that receives these statements must be of the nature of *trust*.

Whenever God announces life and salvation to sinners it is in connection with Christ. 'This is the record, that God hath given us eternal life, and this life is in his Son.' We cannot receive life, or any element of salvation, except by receiving Christ. It has pleased the Father that in Him should all fulness dwell; and the appointed method of supplying our wants is, that first of all we should receive Him, and then receive out of His fulness, even grace for grace. When we truly believe in God's statements respecting the spiritual storehouse, we trust in Christ for all that we need. We feed on Him. A mental habit is formed in us, a law of association, such that whenever our attention is turned to any of our spiritual wants, so often is it fixed on the qualification that enables Christ to supply it. As often as we think of our guilt, so often we think of His atoning blood. As often as we think of our debt, so often we think of Christ as our surety. As often as we think of our unworthiness, so often we think of His merit. As often as we think of our pollution, so often we think of that spirit of holiness that comes forth from Him. As often as we think of our darkness, so often we think of His power to open our eyes and guide us in the way. As often as we think of our unfitness for heaven, so often we think how Christ 'loved His church and gave Himself for it; that He might sanctify it by the washing of water by the word; that He might present it to Himself a glorious church, without spot or wrinkle or any such thing.'

Thus it is that faith in Christ has so much of the nature of trust. But it is trust founded on God's statements respecting Him, and respecting the relation in which He stands to sinners. And hence, too, the remarkable way in which

Jesus was accustomed to offer His blessings. 'Come *unto me*, all ye that labour and are heavy laden, and I will give you rest.' 'If any man thirst, let him come unto me and drink.' 'I am (not I give) the bread of life.' 'I am (not I cause) the resurrection and the life.' All such passages invite to an exercise of trust, and imply that the spirit and habit of trust is essential to the enjoyment of the specific blessings. We get nothing apart from Christ; we get everything in Him and through Him. And hence He is said to be 'made to us of God wisdom and righteousness and sanctification and redemption.'

Few of the questions in the Shorter Catechism are answered with such admirable precision and clearness as that which asks, What is Faith in Jesus Christ? 'Faith in Jesus Christ is a saving grace, whereby we *receive* and *rest upon* Him alone for salvation as He is offered to us in the Gospel.' The operations of faith are summed up in the two things—receiving and resting on Christ—the one the commencement the other the continuation, of one and the same mental process. Like a drowning man, when a plank is thrown towards him, who first catches hold of the plank, and then rests upon it, so the believer first takes hold of Christ, or receives Him, then continues to rest upon Him alone for salvation. The same reasons that impel us to receive Him, impel us to continue to rest on Him. Our helplessness is the same, our personal unworthiness, our liability to fresh outbreaks of sin, our spiritual emptiness, our inability to rise to the heights of heavenly excellence, our vileness in the sight of the Holy God. If we are to be saved at last, we must be looking unto Jesus; if we are to live the life of God's children, it must be by faith on the Son of God, who loved us, and who gave Himself for us.

4. It thus appears that the great function of Faith is to unite us to Christ. And this it does in two ways;—it makes us sharers in Christ's merit, and it makes us sharers in His life.

It makes us sharers in His merit. It gets

for us the benefit of His whole work of atonement. We are justified by faith, because we thereby lay hold on the atoning righteousness of Christ, and rest on it before God, as the ground of our pardon and acceptance. Faith is thus the hand that receives the righteousness of Christ. We are not justified by faith on the ground that faith is accepted in place of obedience. Neither are we justified by faith on the ground that faith is the germ or active principle of obedience, although it is true that it is so. We are justified by faith because by it we lay hold on Jesus as our Saviour, and close on our part with the great transaction whereby 'God hath made Him to be sin for us who knew no sin, that we might be made the righteousness of God in Him.'

It is not difficult to see good reasons why faith, and not obedience or good works, is the appointed instrument of our justification. 'By grace ye are saved through faith, . . . not of works, lest any man should boast.' This arrangement is admirably fitted to keep us humble, to keep us in mind of our emptiness, seeing that we never can have a true sense of pardon and acceptance without looking away from ourselves to our Saviour. It is marvellous how some men contrive to confound what God has made so separate, and mystify what He has made so clear. We have heard of a minister of the last generation, accustomed to offer the prayer—'May we, by our good works, merit an interest in Christ.' Pretty much as if a company of lepers had prayed, May we, by cleansing ourselves, make ourselves worthy of being cleansed by Christ! Let us fancy what it would have been had union to Christ been made to depend not on faith but on works. If only the best people had got the benefit of Christ's work, and that in virtue of their being better than their neighbours, what a world of Pharisees we should have had! In order to found a plea with God, men would have had to show how good they were. Humility, the very soul of all Christian graces, would have been choked to death. There would have been no casting of crowns before the throne—no company there who had washed their robes and made them white in the blood of the Lamb, no salvation for the chief of sinners, no recovered Prodigals, no Mary Magdalenes, no Sauls of Tarsus, in the company of the Redeemed. But for all this, there is a glorious provision when faith is the bond of union to Christ, and the instrument of receiving His merits. We are taught to seek all our justifying righteousness from above, and in the view of the glorious completeness and brightness of that which is offered to us, all righteousnesses of our own dwindle and shrivel into filthy rags.

Besides making us sharers of Christ's merits, faith makes us sharers also of His life. The emblem of the vine and the branches is verified. The grace of Christ is transfused into our hearts, and the life of Jesus is made manifest in our mortal flesh. It is of the very nature of faith to feast itself on the qualities which it sees in Christ. It has a suction-power, if we may so speak, it draws to itself whatever of value it discovers in Him. For true faith is the fruit of the Holy Spirit, and wherever He is at work He not only takes of the things of Christ and shows them to us, but He enables us to feed on them, and find in them the richest spiritual nourishment. And this is the safeguard against the abuse of faith as the bond of union to Christ. If pardon were something by itself, received by faith pure and simple, without regard being had to works, there would be room for great abuse. Men might have an excuse, or at least a temptation, to continue in sin that grace might abound. But faith being the means of union with a living Person, not the mere instrument of receiving a separate blessing, such an abuse is guarded against where the faith and the fellowship are real. True faith regards Jesus Christ with ever-growing admiration. He is its model, its standard, its joy, and its crown. The closer it comes to Him, the more clearly it sees Him 'fairer than the children of men.' The more it tests His grace, the more glorious does it find Him, and the stronger is the desire to be changed into His image. The eternal decree that at one time seemed so terrible, becomes blessed and glorious when its final issue is contemplated—'whom He did foreknow, he also did predestinate to be conformed to the image of his Son, that He might be the firstborn among many brethren.'

It often happens that persons who are conscious of the feebleness of their faith omit one of the chief means by which it may be strengthened. They often subject their hearts to very rigorous dealings in their eagerness to stir up faith. They cry very earnestly for the Holy Spirit, beseeching Him to breathe into them the spirit of genuine trust. All most commendable and excellent. But sometimes the very means is neglected which the Spirit may be most confidently expected to own,—namely, the deliberate examination of the statements which on God's authority they are called to believe, and the devout study of the qualities that make Christ worthy of their trust. For it is far more likely that faith shall be increased by looking out from ourselves to the great Fountain of Life, and to the record which God has given regarding Him, than by mere efforts to stir the stagnant energies of our hearts, whose prevailing state is but too truly indicated in the confession of the Psalmist—'My soul cleaveth unto the dust.'

X.

THE SPIRIT OF LIFE.

IT is strange that, in this nineteenth century, men should be discussing questions on some of the most essential points of Christianity, which were received without dispute in the earliest ages of the Church. In particular, the question—What is it to be a Christian? what is the essence of Christian life? or, wherein does the true Christian differ vitally from other men? would seem in our day to be the occasion of a variety of opinion never dreamt of in the early Church. It is a question which many in our day think it wrong to submit to any theoretical inquiry, and which they would rather that men should leave in the hazy region of the undetermined. And no doubt theories may be drawn out, and have sometimes been drawn out, to a point which is alike unwarranted and disastrous; and incalculable injustice has been done to some men by excluding them from all part and lot in the Christian society, because they have not fulfilled the conditions of some minute human specification of the Christian life and experience. But we must not be deterred by this gross abuse from inquiring whether we are not taught something in the Holy Scriptures regarding the essential elements of the Christian life, whether there be not presented to us in the Word of God views incompatible with much that floats about at the present day as to what really constitutes one a child of God, a member of the kingdom of heaven, a living branch in the true vine, a lively stone in the living temple. To this inquiry we now desire to draw the attention of our readers, as one of the most important in the whole range of saving knowledge: but before entering on it, we will first notice two forms of opinion to be often met with on the subject, but professing to be derived less from the Word of God than from the conceptions and impressions of men's own hearts.

1. Some persons object altogether to any and every attempt to draw a line between the Christian and the no-Christian, or to define explicitly the essential points either in the state or in the character of the former. According to them, the Christian spirit is a sort of atmosphere universally diffused, which all men breathe more or less; or a subtle force, like heat or electricity, seldom wholly absent, but more predominant in some communities and in some individuals than in others. There is something of good, they say, in the worst characters, and something of bad in the best. The shading off between one character and another is so gradual and imperceptible that it is absurd to attempt to draw a line between them, and to represent all as Christians on the one side of it, and no-Christians on the other. Charity ought to rejoice in the fact that hardly any one is utterly lost to what is good, and to anticipate a time when the good shall everywhere

assert its rightful pre-eminence, and the bad shall die out, or be stamped out, as a foreign element that has somehow found its way into the character. It is a mere waste of time, they say, to inquire theoretically what makes any one a Christian. The doctrine of the last judgment, with its sharply-defined separation of the sheep from the goats, is a mere bugbear for frightening people. Let all fair and honest attempts be made to improve the moral atmosphere—to induce men by reasonable considerations to lead better lives; but as for the notion of a hard and fast line—a rigid twofold division—it is the relic of a barbarous age, a thing to be classed with the fires of purgatory.

2. There are others who cannot assent to such views as these, and who yet come far short of the Scriptural doctrine. Reasoning with those whose opinions have just been expressed, they ask them, Do you make no essential difference between two classes of men, of whom the one are struggling to obey the higher impulses of their

nature, while the other abandon themselves to the lower? May not society be at least roughly divided into these two classes? Are not the members of the one class at great pains to strengthen and promote all impulses and habits of the better kind, while the members of the other class habitually disregard them? Do not the one class watch and check their hearts, try in every way to live conscientiously, cultivate improving society, read books fitted to benefit them, and order their whole lives in accordance with these high aims? Do not the members of the other class habitually violate their consciences, and choose companions, books, or amusements with no view to their improvement, but merely to the gratification of the hour? If this be so, must there not be somewhere a line of separation, and some great differentiating principle, constituting the moral character and standing of some men essentially different from those of others?

The answer which is sometimes given to these questions is of this sort. All men are subject to the action of two kinds of principles, the better and the worse. Good men strive to give effect to their better impulses; bad men yield, often without a struggle, to the lower. Good men strive to be just, truthful, sober, kind, forgiving, generous. It is the blessed property of Christianity to give a great stimulus to these endeavours. Under its genial influences men are enabled to succeed much better in this conflict. The atmosphere of Christianity is infinitely better fitted than any other atmosphere to nourish and strengthen this spirit. Thus it is that those who breathe most fully the atmosphere of Christianity become the best men. The reason assigned for this is, not that Christianity communicates anything to them which may be called a new nature, but that Christian influences powerfully stimulate the better impulses of their proper nature, and raise these to a predominance over the worse. It is not because God's Spirit is given to them in a sense different from that in which He is given to all, but because, having better aims than others, they welcome the

Spirit of Christ more, and make more use of the aid which He offers.

If the friends of Christianity should accept of this position, and claim for religion nothing more than the power of bringing out whatever is good in human nature, and raising it to a predominance over the bad, they would be allowed to live in comparative peace. Few people would have any quarrel with Christianity if this alone were its claim and its aim; and some might anticipate for it a career of most friendly and blessed progress, if it simply offered itself to all men as a ministering angel, whose gentle breath should at once wither all the base and hurtful propensities of their being, and stimulate into bright activity everything pure, honest, lovely, and of good report.

How largely this conception of Christianity and of the nature of Christian influence tinges the literature of the day, and especially the imaginative literature, it is hardly necessary at present to remark. Christianity, in a certain sense, is not reviled as an imposture, or a superstition, but recognized as a friend and helper to man. But too often it is just such a Christianity as we have now referred to; not a Christianity that presents an atonement for man's guilt, and substitutes a new heart for the heart of stone; but a Christianity with a warm and highly-fragrant breath—a Christianity that raises the moral atmosphere ten or twenty degrees, and thus enables virtues to bud and blossom and bear fruit, that would have remained torpid in a colder atmosphere.

This brief exposition of views as to the nature of Christian life, that are only too widely prevalent, may enable us to understand and appreciate more clearly the teaching of the Scriptures. Whatever impressions or conceptions men may form on the subject, these can have no real avail in opposition to the lessons of the Word. But this is just what it is so hard at the present day to establish. Men have such extraordinary and overweening confidence in their own impressions, that they cannot hear of anything that runs contrary to them. It is always hard—at the present day it is peculiarly hard—to enter into the kingdom of heaven as a little child. It is rare to find men ready to sit at the feet of Jesus, listening with circumcised ears, and receiving His words as words of infallible truth. The tendency is to bring everything to the standard of our own sense of fitness, and to receive or reject it as it may or may not bear that ordeal; while to listen to the Word, to bow to the Bible as a divine authority never to be questioned, and never to be rejected, is among the rarest attributes of inquirers at the present time.

In order to prevent misconception as to the real issue, let us note two things, which to a certain extent, but only to a certain extent, coincide with some of the views that have now been adverted to.

The first of these is, that in the character even of men who are not truly 'spiritual,' but only 'natural,' there may be more or less of what, in a sense, is good. They who are evil, according to our Lord, may know 'how to give good gifts unto their children.' There may be many pleasing virtues and amiable dispositions to which the human heart instinctively and most justly gives its approval and admiration. The patriotism that sacrifices everything for its country, the instincts of love, the attachment of children to their parents, and parents to their children, the gentle play of humour, the spirit that disdains injustice or dishonour, the heart that aspires to higher purity and a nobler life, are all, to a certain extent, good and commendable. There is no want of readiness in the Scriptures to acknowledge this natural goodness. Even Ephraim, whom Hosea compares to a guilty harlot, was not without such goodness, but like 'the morning cloud and the early dew,' it passed away. That such goodness even in considerable measure may exist apart from salvation, is made obvious by the striking parable of the Rich Man and Lazarus.

Even in the place of woe the Rich Man retained his affectionate concern for his five brethren. The very flames that tormented him had not succeeded in burning out of his heart that instinct of compassion which revolted from the thought of their also coming into the place of torment. Brotherly love was active even when despair had settled down on himself. Marvellous disclosure of the future! Wonderful glimpse of the possibility of some things being saved even from the most appalling of shipwrecks!

The other thing to be noted is that even such goodness as this is to be traced to God as its fountain. No one doubts this in regard to what may be called the instincts. The instincts of the lower animals with reference to their young sometimes exhibit wonderfully the play of self-sacrifice, and other things akin to high human virtues. No one hesitates to ascribe the origin of these instincts to God. So everything in the human heart that is worthy to be called good in any sense is doubtless to be ascribed to God. It is in virtue of a divine power that even such broken goodness is in man. The fact of its being now both broken and defiled does not affect the fact of its divine origin. Every good gift and every perfect gift is from above, and cometh down from the Father of lights. The power of God moving them in the direction of good is in a sense at work in all men. It is seen in the feeling that disdains a lie, in the self-denial that shares its last crust with a needy neighbour, in the sense of honour that prefers death to disgrace. A celebrated popular writer of the last generation, in a piece of autobiography more plain than polished, tells how on one occasion, when he was in the depths of poverty and distress, his life was saved by the kind and cordial ministrations of a poor female outcast in the streets of London. Why should it be denied, that so far as this poor creature was moved to do the part of the good Samaritan, she was under the impulse of a power from God? Or why should it be denied that all that is kindly or genial in human feeling and noble or graceful in human action, and lofty and pure in human aspiration, comes ultimately from the one source of good, however much, in the course of its passage, it may have lost of the purity and brightness of the fountain, and however vile and unworthy of God's acceptance it may have become in consequence of its contact with human corruption?

Notwithstanding all this, we yet maintain it to be the doctrine of Scripture that no amount of natural goodness constitutes any one a Christian, or a member of the kingdom of God; and that to produce that result, there must be a special action of the power or Spirit of God, different from any that takes place in the 'natural' man.

What but this explains the distinction between the 'natural' man and the 'spiritual'? between those that are 'in the flesh and cannot please God,' and those who are 'in the Spirit'? between those who are not far from the kingdom of heaven, like the young man with great possessions on whom Jesus looked so lovingly, and the publicans and harlots who pressed into the kingdom and were safe? between Nicodemus before he came to Jesus, and Nicodemus after he learned of Him? What else explains the fact that when the Apostles preached to the multitude on Pentecost, they looked on all of them as in one category, as men needing redemption and a new life, to be found in Christ alone? The differences in respect of natural goodness in that great crowd were obliterated by the levelling doctrines of universal guilt and alienation of heart from God, needing in every case to be met by Christ's redemption, and by the renewing power of the Holy Ghost. And are we not all familiar with such language in Scripture as conversion, quickening, regeneration? 'Many are called, but few are chosen.' 'Not many great men after the flesh, not many mighty, not many noble, are called.' St Paul congratulated the Thessalonians because his Gospel 'came to them not in word only, but in power, and in the Holy Ghost, and in much assurance.' The same Apostle tells the Corinthians that he 'was with them in weakness and in fear and in much trembling, and his spirit and his preaching was not with enticing words of man's wisdom, but in demonstration of the Spirit, and of power; that their faith should not stand in the wisdom of men, but in the power of God.' Does this not clearly imply that the blessed impression which he sought to get produced, while preaching to them, could result only from a special action of God's Spirit? and that while he abated no means within his power tending towards such impression, he went to work with the deep conviction, that should that special action of the Spirit not be bestowed, all his endeavours would be in vain?

But we have in Scripture a crucial case, as it may be called, the case of Nicodemus. Most remarkable it was that our Lord should have opened His conversation with him by the words, 'Verily, verily, I say unto thee, Except a man be born again, he cannot see the kingdom of God.' Why of all men should our Lord have made this solemn statement to Nicodemus? There was in him, even amid his timidity, much to be commended. A serious, earnest, religious man, with a great desire for light and truth, a profound anxiety about salvation, with many a good impulse, and day by day, doubtless, performing many an act of homage to conscience and to the law of God. Surely this was the very case, if ever one could be, in which there was need only that his good points should be more fully developed, his errors corrected, and an impulse given to his earnest aspirations for good. Yet it is just to this man that our Lord most emphatically lays down the doctrine that he must be born again. How can this be accounted for but on the principle that there may be much genuine desire for good, and in a sense practice of what is good, without the vital change that marks the member of the kingdom of God ; that in every case of entrance into that kingdom, it is not a tinkering up of the old nature, but the inspiration of a new spirit that takes place ; that to be a Christian is not merely to be more in the habit than most people are of giving effect to the better impulses of one's nature, but 'to be born again, not of corruptible seed, but of incorruptible, of the Word of God which liveth and abideth for ever?'

It is strange that any should deny that this is the doctrine of the New Testament. It is not strange that those who judge of truth by their own impressions of the fitness of things should declare all this to be artificial and unnecessary, and should maintain that the natural influences which are at work in every heart in the direction of good, and which in a sense are divine influences, are alone needed for purifying and elevating the nature of man. But surely the teaching of Scripture to the contrary is as plain as can be conceived: 'If any man be in Christ, he is a new creature; old things are passed away, behold, all things are made new.'

The truth is, that those better impulses which remain partly in the heart of man, and constitute his natural virtue, are the results of a broken connection between him and the One Fountain of goodness. It is as if an artery carrying life-blood to a part of the human body had been cut nearly through, and only such a fragment left as conveyed now and then a drop or two, contaminated moreover by contact with the festering wound, instead of an ever-flowing stream of pure and vital fluid. If a true vital connection between that part of the body and the heart is contemplated, a new artery, so to speak, is needed. So, in like manner, it is in a spiritual sense. No attempts to make the shattered arteries of human nature effectual for carrying life-blood from God to the soul can succeed. It is by a new channel the communication is now to be made. A man must be 'born of water and of the Spirit.' The Gospel of Jesus Christ presents this new mode of bringing human souls into living fellowship with God. This is the Scriptural doctrine of regeneration. It is a new fellowship in the divine life, a new communication between the emptiness of humanity and all the fulness of God.

And this is but a very small part of the case. We have said that in man's nature as it now is, the communication with God has been broken, and anything of or from God that may remain in him is but as it were a few ruinous chips of a lost inheritance. But how much worse is the real state of the case! Man is not only separated from God, but alienated too. His will is not submissive to the Divine will. His inclinations are not in harmony with God's commands. Disorder and corruption pervade his whole heart. Instead of his heart turning to God with that completeness of desire and longing which would enable him to draw everything from Him, it is turned the other way. The things of the world are sweet, and his heart goes without an effort after them; the things of God are unattractive, and only to be thought of under the constraint of conscience. God is not in all his thoughts. Religion is a penance; devotional duties a painful necessity.

To convince men of their need of regeneration, of their need of a fellowship with God which is not of the flesh but of the Spirit, is one of the most difficult but indispensable processes in the Christian religion. It is especially difficult in the case of those who are very careful of any natural impulses towards good which they may feel, and diligent in cultivating and strengthening them. Such persons are apt to become so self-righteous and self-satisfied as to present tremendous barriers to the special grace of the Holy Ghost. They are so satisfied with that which is born of the flesh as to see no need for that which is born of the Spirit. Ignorant of God's righteousness, and going about to establish their own righteousness, they do not submit themselves to the righteousness of God. Indeed, there is no obstruction to the work of grace so serious as a state of self-satisfaction. No heart is less likely to open for receiving the stores of the kingdom of God than that which is well pleased with its own attainments. It is a fearful curse when a man who has in the main lived conscientiously and regularly is thereby lulled into the delusion that he 'has attained, and is already' well-nigh 'perfect.' It is an infinite blessing when his utmost efforts to do right have only shown him the utter insufficiency of his own powers; when all his attempts to restrain the wickedness of his heart have but convinced him what sorry work he can make of it at the best; and when the visions that float before him of a holier and more heavenly life serve only to increase the vehemence of his cries for a Divine righteousness to justify, a Divine Spirit to renew, and a Divine love to bless and satisfy him for ever.

And hence, in bringing about the great change, the first operation of the Spirit is commonly to show men their helplessness. And toward this many things may be made to conspire. A view of their *sin* may be given them, that makes them shudder at the thought that all their life long they have been so regardless of the great God. A view of their *danger* may be given them, that pulls them up, as it were—arrests their attention, makes them tremble at the prospect of the wrath to come. A view of their spiritual *feebleness* may be given them, that makes them feel like children before a giant foe, and forces from the depths of their souls the cry for help. And they may have such a sense of forlornness and friendlessness, such an impression of being aliens and outcasts from all that is bright and glorious in the heavenly kingdom, as to feel as if plunged in a very sea of misery. The soul is now fairly prostrate before God, the spirit of self-satisfaction is humbled, the vessel is emptied of all that is born of the flesh, on purpose as it were to be replenished with that which is born of the Spirit.

Then comes, under the guiding hand of the Holy Ghost, a view of Christ. It may be, in a sense, only the old view—the view that in the letter, so to speak, has long been familiar, but not in the spirit; now, however, shining out with a new lustre, and a penetrating, persuasive light that reaches the very depths of the soul. Christ, the Propitiation, is revealed to them atoning for their sins by His obedience unto death; Christ, the Redeemer, rescuing them from all unholy influences, breaking the chains of their sin, and making them free indeed; Christ, the Purifier, washing them in His own blood from all filthiness of the flesh and of the spirit; Christ, the Teacher, making known to them words of truth and life that shall never pass away; Christ the Guide, the Way, the Truth, and the Life; Christ the Spouse, loving His church and giving Himself for it, that He might sanctify and cleanse it with the washing of water by the word ; that He might present it to Himself a glorious church, not having spot or wrinkle or any such thing. How thoroughly the remedy seems adapted to the disease! How admirably is such a Saviour, if He will but undertake the case, able to remove the manifold curse of sin!

But sometimes, even where there is produced the sense of guilt and helplessness on the one hand, and the view of Christ's grace on the other, there is wanting the mysterious link by which the want of the sinner is actually brought into contact with, or supplied from, the grace of the Saviour. It is not enough that the Holy Spirit act on the *conscience,* convincing of sin; or that He act on the *understanding,* enlightening it in the knowledge of Christ; there is further needed an action on the *will,* disposing and enabling it to embrace Jesus Christ, the Saviour offered in the Gospel. Cases may occur, and they are most distressing while they last, in which the keenest sense of unworthiness and the clearest apprehension of the fitness of Christ are connected with a paralysis of the will, in consequence of which the unhappy sinner stands quivering on the edge of a gulf which he cannot get out of view, and under the very shadow of a Saviour to whose arms he cannot fly. The blessed change comes when the Spirit acts on the *will,* so influencing it in favour of Christ that all hesitation is abandoned, and the soul commits itself to its Saviour. Henceforth He is enshrined in the inmost sanctuary of the heart; the divine life begins in earnest; old things are passed away; all things are become new.

One thing must be very apparent, even from this bare outline—how different real conversion is from what is often supposed. Receiving certain dogmas into the creed—submitting one's self to certain religious forms—altering some of the grosser habits of one's life—becoming more earnest in the battle of conscience against inclination—such is conversion in the view of many: but not such alone is conversion as set forth in the Word of God. The first step towards real conversion is to feel our need of it. Men, even when respectable and moral, get accustomed to so low a standard of living, that nothing but a divine revelation can give them a due conception of the pure and lofty ideal to which they ought to aspire. What is it for a man to awake to the possibility of a divine life in the human soul? What is it for him to discover that the spirit within him is capable of an existence far above mere buying and selling, learning and teaching, loving and being loved in the ordinary sense? Is it a mere fevered dream that mocks him with the thought that it is possible for his soul to be cured of all its disorder, emptied of its meanness and bitterness, turned from its poor, earthly delights to objects of infinite worth, replenished with the pure affections of God Himself, and fitted, as far as a creature can be fitted, for pursuits and enjoyments corresponding to those of the Infinite Creator? Is the vision of such a life a mere mirage—a wild device of some bitter foe, trying how far he can raise him up towards heaven, as birds of prey are said to uplift crustacean animals, to shatter them by letting them fall? Is the whole doctrine of Christ and His redemption, so wonderfully adapted to realize all these soaring visions, the mere shadow of old Hebrew traditions, or the mere product of the speculations of theologians? Impossible! There is a glorious reality in these views of a life that may be, and in these views of the power of Jesus of Nazareth to raise one to such a life.

Only let one come to Him who is the Way to the Father, and all is sure. But how to come? How to get above that moral gravitation that drags the soul to earth, and paralyzes all its efforts to rise heavenwards? One thing is plain—there is no power on earth that can overcome gravitation. In the literal sense there is none, and in the moral sense there is none. The power that overcomes gravitation must have its seat in heaven. From above must come the arm that uplifts man to the higher life. 'Draw me, and we will run after thee.' 'Oh that thou wouldst rend the heavens, that thou wouldst come down!'

Innumerable are the difficulties and discouragements which are obviated by a distinct perception and a firm grasp of this truth. Struggling upwards in their own strength towards the kingdom of God, men find little or nothing to reward their efforts, but are painfully reminded how contrary the movement is to that which is natural to them. But opening our hearts to admit the kingdom of God within, standing at the foot of the ladder to receive what is borne to us by the descending angels, welcoming the grace which is God's gift, and which brings most glory to God when it is received as His gift, we may mount up with wings as eagles, run and not be weary, walk and not be faint. Only then can we work out our own salvation, when God worketh in us both to will and to do of his good pleasure. Let our motto then be, 'Waiting and Working.' Waiting for the divine supplies, and working by means of them. 'Eye hath not seen, nor ear heard, neither hath entered into the mind of man, what God hath prepared for him that waiteth on Him.' 'Wait on the Lord, be of good courage, and He shall strengthen thine heart. Wait, I say, on the Lord.'

XI.

MADE HOLY.

'SIRS, what must I do to be saved?'—the cry of the lost, though prior in point of time, is not prior in importance to this, the question of the saved, 'What must I do to be sanctified?' To be sanctified—in plain English, to be made holy—is, to use the admirable definition of the Westminster Assembly's Catechism, 'the work of God's free grace, whereby we are renewed in the whole man after the image of God, and are enabled more and more to die unto sin and live unto righteousness.' But since—to borrow an illustration from a familiar object—it requires as much skill in contrivance and power in execution to restore the image to a coin from which time has effaced the features as it did to impress it there originally, even so to renew man in the image of God is plainly a work as great and divine as it was to form him in that image at the first. In point of fact, this is a new creation; and to Him therefore who, when creating Adam, said, 'Let us make man in our image,' David turned his face and prayer to cry, 'Create in me a clean heart, O Lord, and renew a right spirit within me!'

He who has lost the image of God is like a man who has lost his life—he has neither the will nor the power to restore it. So far, for instance, as Lazarus' power and will were concerned, his dead body, having neither, would have remained in the grave to the day of judgment: nor had the current of the dead man's blood begun again to circulate, nor his heart to beat, unless the voice, which said, 'Lazarus, come forth,' had been that which, at the beginning, called our world and all others into being. Spiritual is as much as natural life the gift of God: and to raise man from a state of nature into a state of grace, to convert a sinner into a saint, is a work, though it may seem less surprising, not less great and divine than it would be to change a dog into a man, or a man into an angel. St Paul knew this. Therefore he offers no unnecessary prayer at the throne of grace, imposes no unnecessary task on God, and fosters in his Thessalonian converts no unnecessary humility, when he prays on their behalf, 'The very God of peace sanctify you wholly!'—and speaking of God elsewhere to the same church he says, 'Who hath from the beginning chosen you to salvation through sanctification of the Spirit and belief of the truth.' Nor than Him, as through Jesus Christ the God of peace, who accomplishes this work by the effectual operation of His own Holy Spirit—is there any other source of sanctification. None else is recognized in the Scriptures, or realized in the experience of believers.

There are, as I shall afterwards show, means of sanctification. These it is our duty and privilege to use diligently. But we are never to lose sight of this—that, apart from the influences of the Holy Spirit, these are vain; altogether vain; nor able of themselves—to borrow a figure from our Lord—to do more than cleanse the outside of the cup and platter; to whitewash the building, leaving it, however, as much as before, a dismal, doleful sepulchre, full of dead men's bones and of all uncleanness. No mistake can be more fatal than one which people, not outwardly vicious, are very apt to fall into—that, namely, of mistaking, not only reformation for regeneration, but outward propriety of life and conduct for sanctification of the heart. Beware of this—the error, the fatal error, into which the Pharisee fell. Correct—perhaps even strictly correct—in his outward demeanour, fasting twice a week, and giving tithes of all he possessed, he stands well in his own esteem; nor doubting that he held as high a place in God's esteem, when his eye falls on a poor publican who stands afar off, and, beating on his breast, cries, 'God be merciful to me a sinner,' this miserable formalist, this whited sepulchre, gives thanks that he is not such as that man. Ah, could he have seen at that moment the proud, ungodly heart that lay concealed beneath this fair exterior, and could he have heard at that moment the judgment heaven pronounced on his case, how amazed had he been! —as much astonished as Belshazzar, when, from the fiery letters on his palace wall, Daniel read out his doom—' Mene, Mene, Tekel, Upharsin, Thy kingdom is divided; God hath numbered thy kingdom and finished it.' While many may, to their own great loss, neglect the means of grace, let those who use them beware lest, proud of that, satisfied with doing so, they get puffed up with spiritual pride, and stand in the same condemnation as the self-righteous Pharisee. Regularity in prayer and the reading of God's holy word, attendance on public worship and the other ordinances of religion, the practice of the various moralities and charities of life, are commendable, and indeed indispensable; but these cannot create a clean heart, nor renew a right spirit within us. The Ethiopian cannot change his skin, nor the leopard his spots; nor anything these hearts of ours but the grace of God. Without that, without the power and blessing of the Holy Spirit, the means of grace are wells without water, clouds without rain.

The necessity of this great work, a work which has God for its author, man for its subject, and for its object his restoration to the image of God, is plain, almost self-evident. Take a simple illustration. In virtue of her royal prerogative, the Queen may pardon all the criminals—the thieves, robbers, murderers, malefactors, scum and dregs of society—which our prisons hold. Let her do so, and every jail would be at once thrown open. But this, illustrating the adage, that it is not always *right* for people to do what they have a *right* to do, would be justly regarded as a public calamity; and every man who had any regard to the safety of his person and the security of his property would take the opening of the prison-doors as a warning to shut his own. Not only so, but ere we would allow the tenants of the jail to enter our houses and mingle with our families, we should require to be satisfied that their habits and hearts were changed—that the drunkard had become sober, the thief honest, the liar true, the vile pure; that they had undergone, in short, such a change as is pictured forth in this lovely vision of the time, when God shall pour out His Spirit upon all flesh, and 'the wolf shall dwell with the lamb, and the leopard shall lie down with the kid, and the calf, and the young lion, and the fatling together; and a little child shall lead them; and the cow and the bear shall feed, and their young ones shall lie down together; and the lion shall eat straw like the ox, and the sucking child shall play on the hole of the asp, and the weaned child shall put his hand on the cockatrice' den; they shall not hurt nor destroy in all my holy mountain, for the earth shall be full of the knowledge of the Lord, as the waters cover the sea.'

Now suppose that the doors, not of our prisons, but of hell itself, were thrown open—which shall never be, for their worm dieth not, and their fire is not quenched—but suppose they were, would the gates of heaven open to receive its inmates? No. Over them these words stand inscribed, 'There entereth nothing here to hurt or to defile.' The door by which Manasseh and the woman that was a sinner, by which the thief of the cross and Saul the persecutor, have entered into glory, would be shut in their face; as, indeed, from the holy nature of its society, heaven would be the last place where they would seek to be admitted. God would not, and could not, receive such as, though pardoned, were still unsanctified; and from their company every spirit of the just made perfect, even their own father and mother, would shrink with holy horror. If so, it is plain that it is not enough to be pardoned, to be justified. We require also to be sanctified, to be delivered from the power and purified from the love of sin. Glory be to God, this has been provided, amply provided for. We are, as an Apostle says, complete in Christ. He who, by dying in their stead, has delivered His people from the punishment of sin, bestows the gift of His Holy Spirit to purify them from its love and deliver them from its power. Thus, with one hand Jesus closes the gate of hell, and with the other throws open that of heaven; and thus those who believe in Him, who cling to Him as all their salvation, and who seek Him as all their desire, receiving with a title to the 'inheritance of the saints' a meetness for it, shall not only not perish in the lake of fire, but shall enjoy everlasting life in the kingdom of heaven. So, to John's question respecting those whom he saw arrayed in white robes, with crowns on their heads and palms in their hands, the angel replied, 'These are they which came out of great tribulation, and have washed their robes and made them white in the blood of the Lamb; therefore are they before the throne of God, and serve Him day and night in his temple; they shall hunger no more, neither thirst any more, for the Lamb which is in the midst of the throne shall feed them, and shall lead them unto living fountains of water, and God shall wipe away all tears from their eyes.'

In regard to the nature of this work, I remark:

I. Sanctification consists in the mortifying of our sinful nature.

An Apostle says, 'They who are Christ's have crucified the flesh with the affections and lusts;' and it is hardly necessary for me to say that, by the term 'flesh,' he does not mean this mortal body, but that corrupt nature which our first parents transmitted to all their children. Its character may be seen in its works; and what these are, when fully developed, may be read in its awful catalogue—'adultery, fornication, uncleanness, lasciviousnesss, idolatry, witchcraft, hatred, variance, emulations, wrath, strifes, seditions, heresies, envyings, murders, drunkenness, revellings, and such like; of the which I tell you before,' says Paul, 'as I have also told you in time past, that they which do such things shall not inherit the kingdom of heaven.'

Of all natural deaths which man can suffer, or

violent ones which he can inflict, none is perhaps more painful than crucifixion. Struck down by a flash of lightning, or deprived as suddenly of life by any other cause, man dies without a touch of pain. Such an advantage is this to those who have made their 'calling and election sure,' who are ready at any time to meet the bridegroom, that we, not believing in 'extreme unction,' have never been able to sympathize with that passage of the Liturgy which teaches the worshippers to say, from 'sudden death,' as well as from 'battle and murder, good Lord, deliver us!' To a good man sudden death is sudden glory; but for that very reason such a death is not suited to describe sanctification—in other words, the destruction of his depraved and corrupt nature in a child of God. Those, again, who die, as most men do, of disease, suffer usually so much pain as to make it one of the special enjoyments of heaven, that 'its inhabitant never says that he is sick,' that there is no death there. Yet the pain of such death-beds is not very formidable; and it is chiefly because the 'dark valley' opens on another world, and 'after death the judgment,' that many are so averse to enter it. Were men assured that there is no hell there, no punishment there, no place but heaven there, thousands who regard death as the king of terrors, would be as willing as they are now reluctant to die; and, therefore, an ordinary death—apart from the consideration of its solemn issues—is usually attended with so little suffering as to offer no adequate figure of the pain and agony inseparable from the mortifying of the flesh. It is therefore to crucifixion, whose intensely painful and protracted agonies the Apostle himself may have witnessed, that St Paul turns for a figure strong and bold enough to describe the death of sin—that death to which all who are Christ's must of necessity, and, rather than lose Him, will of choice, submit.

Believers are thus spoken of as being '*crucified with Christ*,'—a term that calls up to our minds that manner of death which our blessed Lord endured for us. By the side of the dying, in the last struggles of expiring nature, I have seen the features frightfully contorted, the body frightfully convulsed; but the appalling spectacle had this comfort, that the sufferer was unconscious, happily insensible, as the spirit was breaking out of its mortal tenement, to the throes and pangs of dissolution. Such, however, was not the death which Jesus suffered when, to atone for sin, He took its direful punishment on Himself; and in the great love wherewith He loved us died, the just for the unjust, that we might be saved. Behold the Lamb of God! Loaded with infamy and with the tree, He sinks beneath the heavy burden, and falls exhausted, fainting on the street —unpitied save by some women, who, to the everlasting honour of their sex, bewailed and lamented Him. No kind hands are there to make His bed in His sickness; nor weeping friends to smooth His pillow. Rudely throwing Him down on the cross, cruel and malignant enemies drive the iron through His hands and feet—till, weakened by loss of blood and long-protracted tortures,

He yields to the power of death, and bowing His blessed head gives up the ghost! And what agony His, as raised aloft on the cross, He hung by these torn, tender members!

I do not say, it were too much to say, that all who are Christ's, in renouncing the pleasures of sin, suffer pain to be compared with His, or equal to that of any who die on a cross. There may be such cases. The roots of sin are not drawn out sometimes but by a fearful wrench. We see people who prefer their sins to the enjoyment of health; to the possession of property; to a good reputation; to the regard of friends; to the interests of their children; even to life itself! The poor drunkard, for instance, rather than part with his vicious indulgence, will part with all these, and drain the cup, though at the bottom of it he sees the loss of character, a beggared family, death in this world, and damnation in the next. For him, in some cases, to renounce his habits may require greater resolution than martyrs, who walked with firm step and cheek unblanched, have brought to bloody scaffold or burning stake. All I mean to assert is that, as crucifixion implies not the destruction only, but the painful destruction of the body, so they who are Christ's will destroy the flesh, denying themselves to all ungodliness and worldly lusts, though that should cost them sufferings equal to what he endures who cuts off a right hand; or plucks out a right eye; or expires amid the agonies of a cross.

This should certainly suggest the important practical question, whether we have ever taken our sins, and nailed them to the cross? But the question being, not whether our corruption is destroyed, but whether it is being so? not whether it is dead, but whether it is dying? for men to allege, as some do, that they are denying themselves this or that other sinful pleasure is something, but not enough. The Pharisee himself could do so. He gave thanks to God that he was not an extortioner, nor in many respects as other men. But what will such pleas avail? What would it avail a robber, to plead, and justly plead, that he is guiltless of the crime of murder; or the drunkard, that he is not a thief; or the covetous, that he has committed no overt act of dishonesty; or a man of revengeful temper, that he has not actually injured the property or the person of any who have done him wrong? Sanctification embraces the whole man; and the question is not so much whether we have mortified the flesh in this or in that respect, as whether sin in every form has ceased, I do not say to dwell within us, but to have dominion over us? And if we have been enabled through divine grace, though with sore pain, to deny ourselves to pleasures which we once indulged in—and to deny ourselves to them, not because they destroyed our health, or wasted our property, or had lost their power over us through age or change of circumstances, but because they were offensive in the sight of a holy God, because they dishonoured our blessed Lord, because they wounded our consciences, and because they were ruining, not so much this dying body, as our precious souls—then are we crucifying the flesh. This is to be sanctified, to die to sin, and live to righteousness.

The gradual nature of this work will form the subjects for future remarks; but I may observe, before parting with the figure of crucifixion, that the destruction of indwelling sin, like death on a cross, is not only a very painful, but is also a slow and lingering process. No doubt cases—very remarkable cases—have occurred where the 'old man' was slain by, so to speak, a single blow: the crucifying of the flesh being begun and finished within the brief time a man survives who has been nailed to a cross. It was so with the penitent thief. But his case forms no rule. On the contrary, the exception, here as elsewhere, proves the rule—his conversion and his sudden sanctification, all accomplished within the space of some two or three hours, being as extraordinary an exhibition of divine grace, as the resurrection of the saints in the neighbouring tombs was an extraordinary display of almighty power.

Divines have distinguished, and very properly,

between justification and sanctification. They call the first an *act,* the second a *work* of free grace; and this they do because justification is accomplished in a moment, while sanctification, less like a flash of lightning than the morning light which shines more and more unto the perfect day, advances by progressive stages, and may take even long years to finish. Therefore, it is said in the Westminster Assembly's Catechism— one, I may remark, which, though most in use in Scotland, was chiefly the work of Englishmen— that they who are sanctified are 'enabled *more and more* to die unto sin and live unto righteousness.' Hence they are said to be *crucified* with Christ—the most appropriate of all figures— seeing, as we read in Martyrologies, that some condemned for their Master's sake to their Master's death hung for days in protracted agony, ere they exchanged the cross for the crown of martyrdom.

Experience proves that our depraved and sinful nature is not so easily destroyed as many seem to suppose; especially such as have the unspeakable folly to place their hopes in a deathbed repentance. When the convert has dragged the 'old man' to the cross, and nailed him there, how often does he find that his enemy is not only not dead, but, tenacious of life, seems hardly dying! The 'flesh' wars against the spirit; the 'flesh' makes strong and obstinate resistance to grace: and but that the believer is upheld by God's Spirit, but that God according to His promise fights against them that fight against Him, the 'flesh' would triumph in the end; nor could God's people say, as, blessed be God, with Paul they can, 'We are troubled on every side, yet not distressed; we are perplexed, but not in despair; persecuted, but not forsaken; cast down, but not destroyed.' Alas, how often does the carnal nature, which we had almost hoped was extinguished, revived by the breath of some sudden temptation, flame out anew, like fire smouldering in the ashes! Some besetting sin, long denied indulgence, against which we have prayed, and watched, and wrestled, appears to be dead; the 'old man' hangs motionless, to appearance lifeless, on the cross; when, like the convulsive movement of a body from which bystanders supposed the life was gone, in some bad word, or bad deed, or bad thought, the 'old man' lives again, and the 'new man' learns to his sorrow that the flesh he had crucified is not yet dead.

The entire death of sin—a consummation devoutly to be wished for—is a blessing reserved for the close of life. We cannot indeed be too diligent in mortifying sin, in crucifying every limb and member of the flesh. Still if a man will —as every man should—examine himself and 'prove his own work,' the question is not whether sin is altogether crucified, but is crucified at all? —is whether, though it be not with a perfect hatred, we really hate it?—is whether we are delivered, though not completely, from its power?—is whether it has ceased to *reign*, though it has not ceased to *remain* within us? It is slow work dying on a cross, but slower still dying to sin. No vile serpent, no venomous reptile, so tenacious of life as a bosom sin! However, take comfort, Christians; God will perfect that which concerneth us — a hope which, thanks be to God, shows the believer a Father's reconciled countenance shining on him through the darkest cloud; a hope which will enable you, while confessing with Paul, 'The good that I would, I do not; but the evil which I would not, that I do,' in almost the same breath to exclaim, ' I thank God through Jesus Christ our Lord .... there is no condemnation to them who are in Christ Jesus, who walk not after the flesh, but after the Spirit ! '

II. Sanctification lies in conformity to the mind of Christ.

These bodies of ours are liable to an amazing number of diseases; for, though there is but one way by which we enter the world, there are a thousand doors by which to leave it. So insecure indeed is the citadel of life, it lies open on so many sides to attack, that there are none of our organs but may become the seat of a painful and fatal malady. To protect us, to cure disease, men have ransacked the herbs of the field and the bowels of the earth; but have found in neither what they sought in both, any *elixir vitæ*, any remedy against death, any specific of sufficient virtue to cure all manner of diseases. But such a power resided in the hand of Christ. The cures wrought by its simple touch were as magnificent as they were many. Not less sovereign than sudden in action, it gave eyes to the blind, voice to the dumb, ears to the deaf, motion to the withered arm, rest to the palsied limb, and life even to the dead. In the blessed hands his enemies nailed to the cross the world saw what had been esteemed a dream at length realized—a remedy for all manner of diseases; a cure for death itself. Where Christ was, there was need neither for drugs nor doctors.

And were God to impart the same mind to all men that was in Jesus Christ, equally unnecessary were all the ordinary means of checking and curing our moral diseases. Let God so pour out

His Spirit on all flesh as that all men shall be transformed into the image of Christ, and the father might break his rod; the sovereign lay aside his sceptre; the soldier sheath his sword; justice discharge her courts; and with prison-doors thrown open, and no house-door barred, we should sleep in peace—fearing injury from others as little as we had done from Christ himself. St Paul says, 'Looking unto Jesus, the author and finisher of our faith, who, for the joy that was set before Him, endured the cross, despising the shame, and is set down at the right hand of the throne of God—and let us consider him that endured such contradiction of sinners.' He lived more than thirty years on earth, nor injured any one; accused of many crimes, He committed none; He suffered innumerable wrongs, but never inflicted any; into no eye-did He ever bring a tear, nor send a pang through any heart; shedding blessings around Him wherever He went, He could have crowded the hall of judgment with living evidences of His power and goodness;

nor, though in their thirst for His blood they suborned men to swear away His life, could those to whom Judas betrayed his Master find a single person to convict Him of a single crime.

In every relation of life our Lord presents a perfect example: as a child, He grew in wisdom as in stature; and, subject to Joseph and Mary, He whom angels obeyed, obeyed them—as a man, He went about doing good; consecrating His powers to the glory of God and the happiness of mankind, He was eyes to the blind, and feet to the lame, and life to the dead; He made widows' hearts to sing for joy, and earned the blessing of thousands that were ready to perish—as a master, He was kind, considerate, gentle; treating his disciples more as friends than servants, what a beautiful contrast did His demeanour offer to the haughtiness with which many treat and trample on their inferiors—as a benefactor, He shrunk from ostentation, and, unlike the Pharisees, who, to attract attention and win the praise of men, dispensed their charity to the sound of trumpets, He did good, as the poet says, by stealth; charging those whom He blessed to conceal the name of their benefactor—as a lover of God, He delighted in holding communion with His Father, and made it His meat and drink to do His will—as a worshipper, He, who could best dispense with them, devoutly attended on all the ordinances of religion; though giving life to dead souls through the baptism of His Spirit, He sought baptism by water at the hands of John; and though Himself the object of prayer, He prayed without ceasing, and, often spending the whole night on His knees, gave to devotion the hours which the world gave to sleep — as a sufferer, who can be compared to Him? By that cross where He was dumb, opening not His mouth but to say, 'Father, not my will, but thine be done!' reminding us of those plants that lend sweet odours to the hand that bruises them, yonder where He prays that His murderers might be forgiven, we lose sight of the faith of Abraham, the meekness of Moses, and the patience of Job. Like stars at sunrise, these pale and vanish in the dazzling effulgence of this Sun of Righteousness!

Such was Christ, and sanctification lies in conformity to His temper, mind, and life. In all these things He has set us an example that we should follow His steps; and since we are assured that unless the same mind—though it may be only in the bud, in the seed, in the feebleness of infancy—be in us as was in Jesus Christ, we are none of His, *that* becomes a test of Christian character. Without conformity to Him, we are no more to be called Christians than a body without life is to be called a man. Attire the dead like a bride, and with its crown of flowers and sparkling jewels, the corpse but looks the ghastlier; whitewash the sepulchre, and, full of dead men's bones and all uncleanness, the inside seems the fouler; let Judas kiss his Master, and we recoil the more from his treachery—it appears the baser and the blacker. Even so the form of religion without its power, the body of religion without its spirit, a sanctimonious profession with an unsanctified heart, instead of recommending any to God, only renders them more hateful in His sight. Be assured that it is those, and those only, who reflect Christ's image, and whose hearts are tuned to harmony with His own, that are saved by sanctification of the Spirit and belief of the truth. He who died for His people lives in them; renewing them by His grace, imbuing them with His Spirit, and moulding them into the fashion of His own heavenly image. He so helps them to die to sin and live to righteousness, that they also can use the bold language of Paul and say, 'I am crucified with Christ; nevertheless I live, yet not I, but Christ liveth in me; and the life which I now live in the flesh, I live by the faith of the Son of God, who loved me and gave himself for me.'

Let all Christians, then, seek to purify themselves even as Christ is pure; or, as it is otherwise expressed, seek to be perfect as their Father in heaven is perfect. But this is an object, let me say, that cannot be attained in any measure but by daily, unceasing efforts, as, to use a figure of Scripture, they mount up on eagles' wings. Bird of the keenest eye, bird of the broadest wing, bird of the highest flight, let her suspend her efforts, and she does not hang sustained by her plumage — poised in the empty air. Ceasing to rise, the eagle begins to sink, drawn down from the skies to the earth by virtue of its strong attraction; and to a soul which naturally, according to the words of David and to all experience, 'cleaveth to the dust,' this world offers attractions we cannot overcome but by keeping the wings of faith and prayer in constant play. To be holy, to be meet for heaven, we must cultivate every Christian grace with diligence. God is no patron of sloth and idleness, to do for us what we can do for ourselves. In the cultivation of the soul, as of the soil, we are to be fellow-workers with Him. Sanctification is the work of His Spirit; but the work of His Spirit in co-operation with ours. He holds the helm, but we are to pull the oars. He sends the showers, but we are to plough the field, and sow the seed,—looking up for the blessing, and drawing it down with this prayer of David on our lips, ' Let the beauty of the Lord our God be upon us, and establish Thou the work of our hands upon us; yea, the work of our hands establish Thou it!'

III. I go on now to say that sanctification, while the work of the Spirit, is accomplished through the use of means. There is,—

1. Prayer. In their joys and sorrows, in their trials and triumphs also, the children of Israel, during their sojourn in the wilderness, present a striking picture of the conduct and fortunes of Christ's Church on earth; and in nothing more than the use their history teaches us to make of, and the confidence it teaches us to place in, prayer. We have many remarkable examples of this; and none more to our present purpose than what is related as having occurred in Rephidim. It has been often observed that a season of great privileges is a prelude to great

trials, as if God intended by the one to prepare his people for the other. For example, the three disciples who were honoured to bear Christ company on the mount of transfiguration, were the very three He chose to be the painful witnesses of His humiliation in the garden. Again, the Apostle Paul is called up into the third heavens, to hear and see things of unutterable glory; but he leaves these and the company of angels to be buffeted by a messenger of Satan— a warning to God's saints to carry their honours meekly, and look out for storms on the back of sunshine. So was it with Israel in that valley, where, from a rock cleft by the rod of Moses, a river flowed with life in its welcome streams. Seated on its banks, as the people recalled the misery of yesterday,—the whole camp in mutiny, and mothers fiercely pressing on Moses with dying infants in their arms, and this cry on their lips, 'Water, water, give us water!'—they were probably singing, The Lord hath done great things for us, whereof we are glad! At that moment a storm unexpectedly bursts on their heads. The clash of weapons and shouts of war break on the sweet, peaceful scene. The whole camp resounds now with the cry, 'To arms! to arms!' and seizing their weapons, with Joshua at their head, the braves of Israel sally forth to meet the sons of Amalek, who, approaching the host by stealth, have fallen on it like a roaring whirlwind. Meanwhile Moses—not that he was afraid, or a man either to fear or flee—betakes himself to the top of a neighbouring hill. He had other and better work to do than fight. Joshua fights below; and he stands above, holding aloft the rod that had erst woke the thunders of cloudless skies; turned rivers into blood; and, breaking the power of Egypt like a potter's sherd, cleft both sea and rock asunder. Symbol of prayer, it appeals to heaven for help, and teaches the people to look there for victory. And now, that rod, and the arms which sustain it, appear to govern the varying fortunes of the battle. As it stands erect, or falls through the weariness of Moses' arms, so rise or fall the scales of victory. And so, from morning to noon, the tide of battle swaying from side to side, when Moses' arms are up Israel prevails; when they sink, fortune changes sides, and Amalek prevails. The battle was fought by Joshua, but won by Moses. Setting him on a stone, Aaron and Hur, like people engaged in united prayer, join their efforts to sustain his arms. That done, Israel wins every foot of ground; the warriors of Amalek fall at every blow; the fight becomes a retreat; the retreat a rout; till, in the light of the setting sun, Moses descends the mountain to build an altar to the Lord, and in commemoration of a victory won, I may say, by prayer, call it Jehovah Nissi, 'The Lord my banner.'

On the same pivot turns our success in the work of sanctification, so far as concerns our life-long conflict with temptation; the good fight we have to wage with that trinity of enemies— the World, the Devil, and the Flesh. Since prayer supplies the strength and calls down the blessing, therefore everything turns on it; therefore the Apostle speaks of 'praying always;' therefore he urges his converts to ' pray without ceasing.' And as in him whose case, defying the utmost efforts of Christ's disciples, required the presence and power of their Master, there are devils in every man who are not to be cast out but by prayer—earnest and persevering prayer. By way of illustration let us look at two cases— the first teaching us what triumphs are to be won by prayer; the second, what shameful defeats shall follow and punish the neglect of it.

The king of Babylon has issued his impious decree; and this man clothed with a little brief authority has forbidden all men for thirty days, and under penalty of being cast into a den of lions, to pray to any, be it God or man, but to himself. At no time is prayer more needed than when it is forbidden—just as we have never more need to pray than when we are least inclined to do so; when hearts are cold and faith is weak. Bad times require heroes—brave, as well as good men; nor should His people ever stand up more boldly and resolutely for the cause of God than when they are likely in a worldly sense to lose rather than gain by doing so. So Daniel judged. He had never been ashamed to pray; and now, with that decree hanging like a naked sword over his head, he is not afraid to pray. It was no time for such a man as he to seek his closet and shut the door. The time was one requiring faithful men to openly hold up a banner for the truth. So, shaking out its folds in the face of king and princes, friend and foe, death and the devil, Daniel bravely displayed it—throwing his window wide open that all might see him on his knees. Paying an involuntary tribute to his constancy and courage, his enemies watch him; he is seized; hurried from the throne of God to that of a mortal man, and from thence to the den of lions. Hungry and savage, they leap with a roar on their prey, and fight, growling, over his mangled remains? No. Prayer shuts the lions' mouths; gentle as lambs, they gambol around him, or lie crouched in sleep at his feet. Not Amalek, but Israel prevails. There was a man in Scotland once so in love with prayer that he was wont to retire to his old church in the town of Ayr, and spend whole nights upon his knees, till, it was said, they grew hard as the stones he knelt on. But what made the knees callous softened and sanctified the heart; inspiring it at the same time with heroic courage. Fit mate of her, John Knox's daughter, who, on King James offering to set her husband free if he would own the king's supremacy within Christ's Church, replied, as she held out her apron, *I would rather kep his head there,* Welsh rose by prayer above all fear of death. A prisoner in the Bass Rock, where he mingled his psalms with the boom of the breakers that burst on his dungeon walls, that man feared only lest he should not be deemed worthy, like others, to seal his testimony with his blood, and win a martyr's crown.

Now look at another and opposite case. The supper is over; and, pledged in the wine-cup rather to die with Christ than deny Him, the disciples go thence with their Lord and Master. On entering the garden Jesus—entering now into the gloomy shadow of the cross—leaves Peter, James, and John, with instructions to pray. He returns after a little, but it is to find the hands of Moses down—the disciples are asleep. Awakening them, he repeats His injunction, but with no more success; and on a third trial, returns to find them, not praying, but sleeping. They shall sleep no more. The tramp of armed men breaks on the silent night, and torches flash on armour and flicker through the branches of the trees. They are taken by surprise—The Philistines are on thee, Samson! and to them more, in a sense, than to their Master, it 'is the hour and power of darkness.' Jesus triumphed over death, and sin, and hell, entering on the conflict with prayer. But they entered the battle prayerless; and so, after a brief display, a mere flash of courage, they took to flight. And how does Simon, the brave and self-confident disciple who had declared that though Christ's own mother, and the Marys, and all others, should forsake Him, he never would, choosing death rather than desertion—how does he meet this trial? No better, but rather worse than his fellows. We have seen a brave sight—Daniel stand unmoved alike before the wrath of kings and the roar of lions; alas! here—'how are the mighty fallen! the weapons of war, how are they perished! Tell it not in Gath, publish it not in the streets of Askelon!' Peter quails before a woman's eye; and turning his back on that loving Master to whom he had sworn dauntless and deathless allegiance, he now—oh, most cruel and wicked lie!—says, ay swears, 'I know not the man!' Daniel prays, and grace prevails; Peter sleeps, and sin prevails. But who may not, shall not, do the like if prayer be neglected? Let him that thinketh he standeth, take heed lest he fall. Who would mortify the flesh, cast out the devil, burst the bonds of sin, walk in the glorious liberty of sons of God, and, denying themselves to ungodliness and all worldly lusts, at length perfect holiness in the fear of God, must seek their strength, their 'great strength,' in the use of prayer. Prayer is to the Christian what his hair was to Samson; shorn of it, he is feeble as other men.

To be sanctified, therefore, to have our corruptions subdued, to reach greater heights in grace, to grow in the love and the likeness of Jesus Christ, to be mellowing and ripening for the kingdom of heaven, let us pray much; pray often; pray, in a sense, 'without ceasing.' That door is always open, and is open to all. We cannot go there too often, nor ask too much. 'He that spared not his own Son, but delivered him up for us all, shall He not with him also freely give us all things?'

2. Attention to the state of our hearts.

I know an ancient fortress which one brave man could have held against a host. Perched on the summit of a lofty rock, around which the sea goes foaming, and parted from the mainland by a dizzy chasm, over which a narrow arch, hanging like a thread in mid-air, is thrown, that old castle stood in other days impregnable. There was but one way of approach, and *that* such as one man could hold against a thousand. As might be inferred from these words of Scripture, Keep thy heart with all diligence, for out of it are the issues of life, it is otherwise with us. With appetites and passions, each of which may be made an instrument of sin, our hearts lie open on many sides to attack. Take, for example, the most innocent of these appetites, that of hunger—' Give me neither poverty nor riches,' says the wise man, praying as much against the first as the second; because, though happily we know nothing of it, it is difficult for a hungry to be an honest man. The empty sack, as the proverb says, cannot stand upright; and he tempts the poor through this appetite who used it to tempt our Lord Himself—saying to Jesus when He was an hungred, If thou be the Son of God, command that these stones be made bread. In this, as in other ways, Satan tried with his fiery darts every joint of our Champion's armour; and only failed because, as Jesus Himself said, The prince of this world cometh, and hath nothing in me! We cannot say so. Like traitors lurking within a beleaguered city, our natural corruptions are ready to open the gates and betray us to the enemy. Hence he who would keep his heart from evil, keep it pure and holy, must plant a sentinel at every avenue by which sin may find access there—guarding against none more than the little sins, as they are called, that are like the urchins who enter by the window and open the door for bigger thieves. The man of God has his eyes to keep, and so Job said, I have made a covenant with mine eyes—his tongue, and hence the exhortation, Keep thy tongue from evil, and thy lips from speaking guile—his ears, and hence the warning, Cease, my son, to hear the instruction that causeth to err—his feet, and hence David says, I have refrained my feet from every evil way, that I might keep thy word. And since there is no gate of the five senses by which the enemy may not, unless the Spirit lift up a standard against him, come in like a flood, we have need to guard every port, and write over every portal, 'Here there entereth nothing to hurt or to defile.'

The work of grace is carried on within the heart. It is therefore the state of our affections more than our outward conduct that should occupy our chief attention and engage our most earnest prayers. Let me illustrate and enforce this by an analogy. The burning thirst, the flushed cheek, the bounding pulse, the restless nights of fever, are but the symptoms of disease. That thirst physicians may allay by cooling draughts; and opiates may dull the sense of pain, and shed sleep and sweet oblivion on the eyes of the weary sufferer. The symptoms are alleviated, but the disease is not arrested—the evil is but masked, not mastered. And that is all which is achieved in the *reformation* which sometimes passes for *regeneration;* in that outward improvement of habits and decorum of life, which will never supply the place of sanctification in the judgment of a holy, heart-searching God. Man looketh on the outward appearance, but God looketh on the heart. I once heard physicians say, as they stood baffled by the bed-side of one fast posting on to death, We can do nothing now but combat the symptoms. Ominous and fatal words! Divine grace, thanks be to God, does more. Let it reach the heart, and those works of the flesh, which are the outward symptoms of indwelling sin, will ere long pass away, like a plant which, cut at the root, droops, and withers, and dies. It is in the heart the change is wrought for salvation; and there, as a building rises from its foundations, the work of sanctification is carried onwards and upwards to perfection. Cleanse this fountain, and purity will flow in all its streams. Let our heart be turned heavenward, and our members and affections, our powers, and time, and influence, will all follow and obey its movements—as from stem to stern, from her keel that ploughs the wave to the masts that rake the sky, a ship obeys the hand of the steersman and movements of the helm. Who, therefore, would grow in grace, would die daily to sin, would live daily to righteousness; while they strive to keep their hands from doing, and their ears from hearing, and their lips from speaking evil, let them strive above all things to keep their hearts with all diligence, since out of them are the issues of life.

3. Living separate from an ungodly world.

With all the world in His choice, God placed His ancient people in a very remarkable situation. On the north they were walled in by the snowy ranges of Lebanon; a barren desert formed their eastern boundary; far to the south stretched a sterile region, called the howling wilderness; while the sea—not then, as now, the highway of nations, facilitating rather than impeding intercourse—lay on their west, breaking on a shore that had few harbours and no navigable rivers to invite the steps of commerce. Such a position rendered frequent and familiar intercourse on their part with heathen nations difficult, if not impossible. Other circumstances also tended to isolate the Israelites. The words of their law read every Sabbath, and the blood of the passover sprinkled every year on their doors, kept alive the memory of old wrongs—reminding the Hebrews of what their fathers had once suffered in the land of Egypt. This was calculated to alienate them from the Egyptians, their neighbours on the south and west; and the Egyptians, on the other hand, were not likely to regard the Israelites with a friendly eye, seeing how, in the oxen and heifers of their sacrifices, they offered up the very gods of Egypt on the altars of the God of Israel. Their other neighbours were the Philistines and Edomites. The first, the surviving remnant of nations whose lands Israel had seized, had old defeats and the blood of their countrymen to avenge; while the second, the children of Esau, were ready when ever opportunity offered, to renew their father's quarrel with Jacob, and fall on Jerusalem with the sword, and cries of Raze it, raze it to the ground! Thus, besides their geographical position, the relations of God's people to the nations around them were singularly well calculated to keep them a separate and make them in a sense a holy people; to expose them to the enmity rather than win for them the friendship of the world—a position which our Lord pronounces, and Christians find in their experience to be, the safest and therefore the happiest of the two. 'When men persecute you and hate you,' said our Lord, 'and say all manner of evil against you falsely, rejoice, and be exceeding glad, for great is your reward in heaven.'

England's great dramatist speaks of finding 'sermons in stones, tongues in trees, and books in the running brooks,'—and may we not find a great truth in the very position in which God placed his chosen people? It certainly teaches us that to be holy, or sanctified, we must be a separate people—living in the world, but not of it—as oil, that may be mixed but cannot be combined with water. Nor was this the only way God took to teach His people, and through them us, this lesson. In our looms, for example, nothing is more common than to work up into the same web materials of different textures—wool from the snowy flock, with flax from our own, or cotton from foreign fields; nor is it uncommon for our farmers to sow different kinds of seeds in the same field; and occasionally in our country, and very often abroad, we see different kinds of animals yoked to the same plough or cart. Very harmless customs, yet strictly forbidden to the Jews by these laws of Moses—Thou shalt not sow thy field with mixed seeds, neither shall a garment mingled of linen and wool come upon thee; thou shalt not plough with an ox and an ass together. And what spiritual lesson were these regulations intended to teach, but this, that it is not safe for those who would live godly to associate with the ungodly; that, if we would not be partakers of other men's sins, we must live, as far as lies in us, separate from their society?

'Come out from among them, and be ye separate, and touch no unclean thing: and I will receive you, and will be a Father unto you, and ye shall be my sons and daughters, saith the Lord Almighty.'

We have seen an adroit debater seek by the use of ridicule to throw contempt on what he could not refute: and this has he who is fertile in wiles done with the duty that lies on Christians to live separate from an ungodly world. Satan has sought to make it ridiculous. In the hermits of old times, in the convents and monasteries of Popery, where roam, in the words of Milton,

> 'Embryos and idiots, eremites and friars,
> White, black, and gray, with all their trumpery;'

and in the seclusive, not to say sour and exclusive, habits of some good but narrow-minded Protestants, he offers us a caricature of this duty and God's truth.

It would neither promote our sanctification, nor the glory of God, nor the good of others, to withdraw altogether from worldly society. To 'depart from evil' is but a part of our duty; we are also to 'do good.' 'Pure religion and undefiled' walks not in solitude; her hands are employed providing the orphans bread; her feet are found at the widow's door; her steps are even sometimes turned to haunts of vice; her visits are paid not so much to the great and noble as to the fatherless and widows in their affliction; and following our Lord, nor shrinking from the touch of guilt, she goes forth to seek and save the lost. The proper station for a life-boat is not the quiet lagoon or land-locked bay, but the shores of a stormy coast. But though true religion seeks to strengthen her graces by exercise, and thus effectually promote the work of sanctification, that is a totally different thing, both in its intention and results, from voluntary association with the ungodly; from courting the company and cultivating the friendship of such as are not the friends but the enemies of God. It is not safe, as Lot found to his cost, to live in Sodom. Who can touch pitch, and not be defiled? Sailors give a wide berth to shoals and whirlpools, and we shall find it safest and most for our sanctification to keep away from seductive influences—not so much as venturing into the stream which has carried off their feet many who fancied they could stem its torrent. How often have God's people learned to their sorrow that worldly society—cooling if not quenching their love, blunting the fine edge of a renewed conscience, and checking their growth in grace—has done them far more ill than they ever did it good. Who walks, as we do, in slippery places is in great danger of backsliding; who throws himself into a crowd is more likely to be borne along with the current than to stop it; and who even bravely and nobly attempts to save the drowning must be on his guard lest, locked in their deadly embrace, he sinks to perish along with them.

It is impossible to altogether escape the temptations which the world presents; in that case, a man, as Paul says, must needs go out of the world. This has been tried. But in vain have pious dreamers fled the haunts of men, expecting in the depths of untrodden forests, in caves and lonely deserts, to enjoy uninterrupted communion with God. Alas, they carried with them in the corruption of their own hearts what often proved the worst of company; nor there did they escape him who pursued our Lord Himself to the solitudes of the desert. But suppose that hermit's cell or cloistered convents offered a perfect protection from evil in every shape and form, it were not the duty of God's people to withdraw from the world. It has need, much need of them. 'Unless these abide in the ship, ye cannot be saved.' Saints are the salt of the earth, and if the salt be withdrawn, how is corruption to be checked? Saints are the lights of the world; but lights are not kindled in empty halls and unpeopled solitudes. They burn where houses stand thick and crowds throng the busy streets: or shine out at the harbour mouth through the night and tempest— guiding lights by whose welcome gleams the sailor, leaving storms behind, steers his bark into the desired haven. Let such be the aim of God's people. Living for their sanctification, separate in a sense from the world, and moving, like the stars above it, in a loftier sphere, let them shine with the lustre of holy and useful lives, that others, seeing their good works, may glorify their Father which is in heaven.

4. The hope of glory.

Hope is a medicine on which physicians place great dependence; nor is there almost any symptom they are more prompt and anxious to combat than the depression of mind which, prostrating the vital powers, goes to produce the very evil that it dreads. Imparting courage, and also strength, firmness to the troops who receive, and energy to those that make the charge, hope has braved the face of death, and won proud victories on many a battle-field. In almost every position of life hope is the prelude of success; as *hopeless*, on the other hand, may be justly regarded as equivalent to *helpless*. No hope, no effort—as observed in the demeanour of an unhappy Indian who, caught in the current, perished in the Cataract of Niagara. Wearied with the chase and asleep, or forgetful of his peril, he had allowed his canoe to drift into the rapids, nor awoke to his danger till the current was sweeping it along with an arrow's speed. Roused at length by the shouts of terrified spectators, he sprang to his feet, and, looking around him, took in all the danger at a glance. But he seized no oar, nor raised a cry, nor made an effort to reach the bank. With the courage of his race, and the calmness of despair, the savage bows to his fate; resumes his seat; and, folding his arms, awaits the moment, when, borne over the fall, he is buried in its boiling gulf. Hope had fled.

The Word of God furnishes two cases strikingly illustrative of the influence of hope on the one hand, and of hopelessness on the other. I refer to those of Saul and David, when each went forth to meet the Philistine. It needed no familiar spirit, nor prophet from his grave, nor accursed witch that night Saul repaired to her hut in Endor, to foretell the disasters of the coming day. Prostrate at her feet, abandoned of God and of hope, rejecting both food and comfort, Saul was already conquered. In his crushed hopes and heart coming events cast their shadow before. Paralyzed by despair, he was incapable of such efforts, either of body or mind, as the time and his danger required. Ready to fall before the Philistines as a noble oak whose roots have been severed by the axe before the first blast of the rising storm, he had not a chance in the coming battle.

What a contrast to this scene the day that saw David, in the sight of two armies that hung on opposing hills, hastening with eager eye, and flying locks, and elastic foot to meet the giant! Hope was in his bounding step; and sounds to my ear like the blare of a battle trumpet in his reply to Goliath, 'Thou comest to me with a sword, with a spear, and with a shield; but I come to thee in the name of the Lord of Hosts, the God of the armies of Israel, whom thou hast defied; this day the Lord will deliver thee into mine hand, and I will smite thee and take thine head from thee; and I will give the carcase of the host of the Philistines unto the fowls of the air, and to the wild beasts of the earth, that all the earth may know that there is a God in Israel: the battle is the Lord's, and He will give you into our hands.' Brave speech! this was the voice of hope, of heaven-born hope. Sustaining David's heart, giving sight to his eyes and imparting strength to his arm, as, whirling the sling around his head, he launched the messenger of death right to the mark, that hope was the omen, and under God the means of victory.

And so it is in the Christian's conflict with sin; and indeed in all the work of sanctification. Hence, not for our peace only, but for our purity also, the importance of a 'lively hope,' of making our calling and election sure. In spiritual as in earthly things, there is great strength in hope; and, therefore, God's people are carefully to cultivate that grace. Carefully avoid everything that could cast a doubt on your salvation; throw you into a state of spiritual darkness; and bring you, as David seemed to have been brought by his great sin, to the very borders of despair. A well-grounded hope that, having been made new creatures in Jesus Christ, we are His—that with our names, though unknown to fame, written in the Book of Life, we have grace in possession and heaven in prospect—that after a few more brief years, pure as the angels that sing before the throne, we shall be brought with gladness into the palace of the King, to be like Christ, and with Christ, seeing Him eye to eye, and face to face—such hopes are powerful springs of action. The source of a peace that passeth understanding, nothing could be better calculated to wean our affections from the world, and deepen our abhorrence of sin, and inflame our desires to be holy as God is holy.

IV. Sanctification is a progressive work.

A connoisseur in painting, so soon as the dust of years and neglect is wiped from a fine old picture, can tell whose hand laid these colours on the canvas—the works of each of the great masters having a character of their own. In like manner an antiquarian, though history is silent on the subject, and no date stands carved on the crumbling ruin, can tell when this tower was built, or that arch was sprung—the architecture of every age being marked by features peculiar to itself. And to pass from small things to great, so distinguished are God's works by features all their own—evidences of divine goodness, power, and wisdom—that a Bedoween, when asked how he knew there was a God when he had never seen Him, had good reason to look with surprise on the sceptic, and reply, as he pointed to a footprint in the sand, 'How do I know whether it was a man or camel that passed my tent last night?'

Among other features impressed on all the works of God, none is more distinctly marked than their progressive character. It was step by step, and day by day, not all of a sudden, that our world was constructed, and creation finished —with man, his Maker's image, and his crowning work, standing on the summit of the pyramid. The Providence, also, that sustains and governs the world is no less distinctly marked by progress. Babes grow into men; seedlings into trees; the gray dawn into the rosy morn; the morn into the blaze of sunshine; and the green blades that spring from dull clods into the golden sheaves of autumn. Nothing in nature starts at once into maturity—neither the fish of the sea, nor the fowls of the air, nor the flowers of the field, nor the trees of the forest. Nor is man himself, in respect of either soul or body, exempt from this imperial law. Going away to push your fortune in the world, you leave an infant in your mother's arms, and return after long years of absence to hail the blue mountains of your native land as they rise above the wave. Hastening homewards, you stand once more amid the dear and well-remembered scenes of other days. The same trees wave over the house, the same stream with its daisied banks runs murmuring by the door; and, though time has silvered their heads, and written wrinkles on their brows, you at once recognize the faces and are locked in the arms of happy and beloved parents. But who is he that stands there, in strength and stature a mighty man?—but the infant you left hanging helpless on a mother's breast. And thus, without any previous knowledge of the matter, and looking only at God's works of creation and providence, we could predicate that sanctification, one of the greatest of His works, would also be one of progress—giving us no more reason to expect that a sinner on his conversion would suddenly grow up into a perfect saint than a seedling into a perfect tree, or the field sown to-day be to-morrow flashing with the sickles and joyous with the song of reapers. Grace has its dawn as well as day; grace has its green blade, and afterwards its ripe corn in the ear; grace has its babes and its men in Christ. With God's work there, as with all His works 'in all places of his dominion,' progress is both the prelude and the path to perfection. Therefore we are exhorted to grow in grace, and in the knowledge of our Lord and Saviour Jesus Christ —to lay aside every weight and the sin that doth more easily beset us, and run with patience the race set before us—to run so that we may obtain —to go on to perfection, saying with Paul, What things were gain to me, those I counted loss for Christ; yea, doubtless, and I count all things but loss for the excellency of the knowledge of Christ Jesus my Lord. I count not myself to have apprehended; but this one thing I do, forgetting those things which are behind, and reaching forth unto those things which are before, I press towards the mark for the prize of the high calling of God in Christ Jesus.

This is a view of sanctification well calculated to strengthen feeble knees and hold up arms that are ready to hang down. I am a great sinner— my head is dark and my heart is dead—my feet are ever slipping—when I would do good, evil is present with me; what I would I do not, and what I would not that I do! has been the complaint of the godly. And as a native of the plain, who climbs some Alpine summit, on finding, when he has reached the first height, that another rises before him, and after it another, and still another, each towering higher into the sky, is ready, under the depressing influences of disappointment and fatigue, to throw himself on the ground and abandon the task in despair, so, thus complaining and confessing, God's people have been ready to fall into despondency and, writing hard things against themselves, lose the blessed hope of being ever wholly sanctified.

But why should you be cast down, or your spirits disquieted within you? 'It is good that a man should both hope and quietly wait for the salvation of the Lord.' Descrying the day in the dawn, the man in the stammering babe, and in the seedling the stately tree with roots rifted in the rock and giant arms thrown out defiant of the storm, let His people rejoice in the Lord, and joy in the God of their salvation. It is not possible for them to employ language humbler than that of St Paul, the great Apostle of the Gentiles. He reckoned himself 'the chief of sinners, and less than the least of saints'—that he had not attained, or was yet perfect. But did he therefore go mourning all the day long, wearing a face of gloom and hanging his head like a bulrush? No. He went out to work, expecting a blessing on his labours; he went down to battle confident in God, and therefore confident of victory. They cast him into the inner prison, and he passed the night singing psalms of praise; they hunted him like a partridge on the mountains, and he rejoiced in tribulation; they, both the heathen and his own countrymen, sought to overwhelm him with persecutions, and amid perils and sufferings many he rose, like the ark, buoyant on the top of the flood; Death shook his grisly hand at him, and he defied the king of terrors—this the source of his joy and peace, of his unwearied energy in work and dauntless intrepidity in danger, the confidence that He who had begun a good work in him would carry it on to the day of the Lord Jesus. No cloud on his brow nor in his sky, I am persuaded, he exclaimed, that neither life, nor death, nor angels, nor principalities, nor powers, nor things present, nor things to come, shall be able to separate me from the love of God, which is in Christ Jesus our Lord.

This confidence is 'the inheritance of the saints'—of all the saints. The blood of Jesus has lost none of its virtue, nor His Spirit any of its power; the fountain of grace is not exhausted, nor is the edge of the sword of the Spirit of God either rusted by age or blunted by use. To-day, the sun in heaven shines as bright as when his old fires first began to burn: and so does that better Sun, the Sun of Righteousness, which sheds healing in its beams—to-day, the wind sweeps field and forest with wings as strong and free as when first it stirred in gentle breezes or tossed in storms the palms of Eden: and now not less free and full than ever that Spirit which is as the wind that bloweth where, and when, and how it listeth—to-day, the great sea, 'where go the ships,' after receiving, for long ages, into its capacious bosom the mud and mire, the decay and death of a thousand rivers, is as pure as when its billows first broke their snowy heads on the shores of our new-born world: and so, though ten times ten thousand and thousands of thousands have washed away their guilt in the blood of Christ, are the fountains of grace and salvation. For deliverance from the love and power, as well as the guilt, of sin, we are 'complete in Christ.' In this confidence, though with fear and trembling, let us work out our salvation; God working in us both to will and to do of His good pleasure. Seeking the aids of the Holy Spirit, let us aim at perfection. Let every day see some sin crucified, some battle fought, some good done, some victory won; let every fall be followed by a rise, and every step gained become, not a resting-place, but a new starting-point for further and higher progress; and looking over the gloomy confines of the grave to the glory that lies beyond, let us meet our last hour and last enemy, when they come, calm 'in the sure and certain hope of a glorious resurrection'—this our confidence, that He who hath begun a good work in us will carry it on to the day of the Lord Jesus; and will, while mourning friends receive our parting sigh, bring forth the 'headstone'—all the angels of heaven and all the saints in glory shouting, 'Grace, grace unto it!'

XII.

THE SACRAMENTS.

THE origin of the word 'Sacrament' is peculiar. It occurs nowhere in the Bible, but, like the word 'Trinity,' is of purely ecclesiastical origin. In the well-known translation of the Scriptures into Latin, commonly called the 'Vulgate,' whenever the word *mysterion,* or *mystery,* occurs in the original Greek, it is rendered by the Latin *sacramentum.* Sacramentum means generally a thing possessing sacredness, but hidden or concealed; and more specifically the oath which Roman soldiers used to take that they would be faithful to their country and obey their general. The application of the word to certain ordinances of the Christian religion, arose from the idea that there was a hidden sacredness about them. There was in them a mysterious relation between certain outward acts and the most solemn and awful truths of the Christian faith. This notion of mystic sacredness, while not destitute of a certain foundation in the Word of God, has been enormously exaggerated, under the influence of certain ecclesiastical tendencies. In fact, the mysterious aspect of the sacraments has often been so presented as to do incomparable damage. Under the impression of an inseparable connection between certain outward acts, and the highest blessings of the kingdom of God, men have been encouraged to attach to the sacraments by themselves an importance as disastrous to their spiritual welfare, as it is destitute of foundation in the Word of God. And, as often happens, this extreme has been followed by a corresponding reaction. From the enormously exaggerated value attached by some to the sacraments, others have recoiled to the opposite extreme. In their view the sacraments, so called, are of little value. All saving blessings depend on faith in the Word of God. It is the spiritual reception of divine truth that alone is of saving value. The sacraments, according to this view, are little more than acknowledgments of belief and badges of profession;—and any notion of a hidden sacredness, or a hidden relation in them to the chief blessings of salvation, beyond what this view implies, is a mere devout imagination.

It is between these extremes that we conceive the truth to lie. With the supporters of the latter view we hold, and hold very strongly, that the spiritual reception of revealed truth, especially the truth regarding Christ and His salvation, is the only link between the sinner and the Saviour, the only mode of receiving into our possession the blessings of the kingdom of heaven. But it by no means follows from this that the sacraments are of little use. The sacraments may, and we believe do, render essential service when God's blessing rests on them, in promoting the believing reception of saving truth, in enabling us to grasp Christ and His blessings, to receive and rest upon Him alone for salvation. It is this view of the sacraments, as essential aids to faith, that finds most favour in the churches of the Reformation. The two distinctive views, which may be termed the one Popish, the other Protestant, are first, that a certain store of saving grace has been deposited in the sacraments, and is, by the very act, communicated to the recipient of them when they are rightly administered; and second, that the sacraments are simply channels of communion with Christ, means of promoting the Christian graces,—especially of calling into exercise the faith that appropriates Christ and feeds on Him; and that, in these respects, a special blessing rests on them when rightly received. The main difference between the two systems is, that according to the one, there is a store of grace in the sacraments, according to the other, the only store of grace is in the person of Christ. By the one you get grace when you receive the sacrament; by the other you get grace only when by faith you feed on Christ. This last position is eminently characteristic of all truly Protestant Churches. The Protestant doctrine is, that the only deposit of grace is in the living Christ. The soul that is to taste of saving blessings must in every case be in personal communion with Christ, and that personal communion can take place only in the exercise of faith. No part of saving grace has been sent away from Christ to sacraments or any other ordinances. 'It hath pleased the Father that in Him should all fulness dwell.' Sacraments therefore belong to the same category as the preaching of the truth. They serve to exhibit Christ,—to exhibit Him in most solemn and precious lights;—when they are received in faith, the blessing of God rests on them; they then seal or confirm the blessings which they exhibit, and they convey the blessings which they seal. It is not, as Vinet remarks, that the word becomes a rite, but the rite becomes a word. The sacraments are symbols and seals of saving truth; and they are made effectual to salvation, 'not from any virtue in them, nor in him that doth administer them; but only by the blessing of Christ, and the working of His Spirit in them that by faith receive them.'

But what are the ordinances to which the name of Sacraments is applied, and for what reason is it so used? In the Protestant Church the term is restricted to the two ordinances of Baptism and the Lord's Supper. In the Church of Rome it embraces besides, confirmation, penance, extreme unction, ordination, and matrimony. We do not mean to enter here on the controversy with Rome on this point. We simply remark that the name is restricted by Protestants to Baptism and the Lord's Supper, because these two ordinances alone are held to possess the features that entitle them to the name.

1. In a sacrament, there is a certain outward act or ceremony, which is a sign, picture, or representation of some of the blessings of salvation.

This is obviously true of the two ordinances of the Old Testament which are commonly ranked as sacraments, Circumcision and the Passover, as well as of those of the New. In administering circumcision, a certain act or ceremony was performed, which act, from its very nature, was a representation or sign of the truth, that whatever is born of man is polluted, and needs as it were to be cut off—in other words, that the whole nature of man is corrupt, and that it needs to be suppressed, and succeeded by a holier. Circumcision, in its very nature, was thus a sign or representation of the mortifying of the old man, with his affections and lusts—putting off the old man and putting on the new. And hence, in writing to the Colossians (ii. 11) the apostle reminds them that through Christ they had experienced the inward reality of which circumcision was the outward representation—' in whom also ye are circumcised with the circumcision made without hands, viz., in putting off the body of the sins of the flesh, by the circumcision of Christ.' The Passover, again, was an evident and a very significant representation of salvation through Jesus Christ. Both in itself and in the circumstances in which it was instituted, it was fitted to shadow forth the way of salvation. On the night of its institution, the Angel of the Lord passed over the houses of the Israelites, on whose door-posts the blood of the lamb was sprinkled, and left the deadly token of his visit on the person of every Egyptian firstborn. How significant was this of the difference between a state of salvation and a state of condemnation! The wail of distress issuing from every dwelling of Egypt, the joyful sense of deliverance brightening every Hebrew countenance—what expressive symbols these were of the feelings of the two great classes of men on the day of judgment! In the sacrament of the Passover, *the manner of partaking* was not less expressive. A meal was furnished for a whole household from a slain lamb, roasted whole, which was served with bitter herbs to the members of the family in a standing posture, with their shoes on their feet, and their staves in their hands;—shadowing forth how Christ our Passover is sacrificed for us; how His flesh and blood, received in faith, become the meat and drink of the soul; and how it is as pilgrims and strangers, passing from a house of bondage to a heavenly home, that we should eat this feast, and receive this salvation.

When we turn to the two sacraments of the New Testament—Baptism and the Lord's Supper, we find that they too very obviously furnish representations of the leading blessings of salvation. Thus Baptism, bringing the person baptized into immediate contact with water, represents the close personal connection into which Christ is brought with the soul of the believer, and the manner in which the grace of God, which bringeth salvation, purifies men,—constrains them to live soberly, righteously, and godly in this present world. Pure water poured on us in the name of the Father, Son, and Holy Ghost, represents at once our native pollution, and testifies to a method of removing that pollution, in which Father, Son, and Holy Ghost concur. In the sacrament of the Lord's Supper, again, the broken bread and the poured out wine are plainly fitted to represent the sacrifice of Christ, while the eating and drinking of these very significantly indicates the emphatic way in which His sacrifice is appropriated, the closeness of the union between Him and the believer, and his entire dependence on Christ for the sustenance of his spiritual life. In the words of one of the greatest of theologians—' Baptism testifies that we are washed,—the Supper, that we are redeemed. Ablution is figured by water,—satisfaction, by blood. Both are found in Christ, who, as John says, came by water and by blood, that is, to purify and to redeem. . . . This sublime mystery was illustriously displayed on the cross of Christ, when water and blood flowed from His sacred side; which, for this reason, Augustine justly termed the *fountain of our sacraments.*' (Calvin.)

2. Another feature of the ordinances called Sacraments is, that they are *seals* or *confirmations* of the blessings which they represent. They can-

not make the blessings more certain than they would otherwise have been; but they convey the notion of their certainty more impressively to men. Thus we are told of circumcision, that it was to Abraham a seal of the righteousness which he had by faith, being yet uncircumcised. In other words, it was to Abraham a confirmation of the truth that in consequence of his faith he was accounted righteous in the sight of God. A man of like passions with ourselves, the mind of Abraham might have been clouded with doubts, whether the covenant would really be fulfilled to him—and in particular, whether he would really be accepted through his faith by the great Judge or no. Circumcision was God's seal, testifying that the covenant would stand fast and that he would be accepted. As often as it was administered, it was equivalent to a solemn assurance from God that all would be made good to him; it was as if he had heard God's voice declaring, 'The mountains shall depart, and the hills be removed, but my kingdom shall not depart from thee, neither shall the covenant of my peace be removed, saith the Lord that hath mercy on thee.'

The Christian ordinances, Baptism and the Lord's Supper, are seals in a similar way. They are divine attestations to the provisions of the new covenant, divine assurances that all these provisions shall be made good. But let us mark to whom this assurance is conveyed. Not to every one who happens to receive the sacrament. The fact of any one being baptized, or receiving the Lord's Supper, is not necessarily to him a seal or assurance of salvation. It is so only when he is a believer. Circumcision would have assured nothing to Abraham if he had not previously believed the promise of God. It was not an assurance to Abraham absolutely, but to his faith. The seal was not attached, so to speak, to Abraham as an individual, but to Abraham as a believer. The case is similar with the New Testament sacraments. They are not seals absolutely to every one who receives them, but only to those who have faith. Wherever there is a heart looking to Jesus for salvation, looking to the 'water and the blood' at once for cleansing and for purification, they assure that heart of the blessings which it seeks. They are God's seals or attestations to the faith of that soul—material guarantees, as it were, of the blessings of the future, pledges of the payment in full of the blessings that have been promised when the moment shall have come at which the bill falls due.

It is of the greatest possible practical moment to bear in mind that the sacraments seal nothing but condemnation where there is not faith in Christ, and in the benefits of redemption through Him. Wherever this fact is duly considered, it will discourage the habit of resorting to the sacraments, without regard to the state of mind of the person receiving them. Of what avail can the reception of the sacraments be to one who has not opened his heart to Christ, and who has no real faith in the blessings of his purchase? Can it be imagined that the mere reception of these ordinances compensates for the careless or unbelieving heart, or that God regards the mere bodily service as equivalent to the holy trust of the regenerated soul? The supposition is as wild as it would be to suppose that by possessing ever so many impressions of a rich man's seal, one was assured of inheriting his wealth. The seal is nothing apart from the document to which it has reference. Sacraments assure nothing, apart from the covenant of grace, and faith in that covenant. If one should suppose that going to the Lord's table will save him, though he has no real faith in Christ, and hardly knows what redemption means; if a parent, receiving baptism for his child, fancies that it will bring a blessing, although he, as representing the child, knows and cares nothing of the salvation in the name of the Father and of the Son and of the Holy Ghost of which that sacrament speaks; or if a grown-up person, who had been baptized in infancy, should persuade himself that his baptism had done him some mysterious good, though meanwhile he neglects the Saviour to whom he was presented, and tramples on the covenant in which the salvation is offered,—such persons are practising a miserable deception. They trust to a seal which can seal nothing to them, because they destroy the only ground or surface to which the seal can have an attachment. It is as if a company of miners should suppose that because they grasp a certain rope they shall be drawn to the surface, although they have detached the end of the rope from the machinery by which alone it would have accomplished its purpose.

3. There is a third property of the ordinances which we call sacraments,—they are channels by which the blessings which they represent and seal are actually conveyed or applied to believers.

Besides being visible representations of the blessings of redemption, and seals or pledges of the certainty of these blessings to all who partake of them in faith, they serve, with God's blessing, actually to communicate them, or some of them, to their souls. The sacrament of the Supper furnishes the most intelligible illustration of this remark. Not only does that sacrament represent or picture forth the manner in which sinners are saved through the sacrifice of Christ; and not only does it confirm the promise of God that all who take Christ as their Saviour shall come to salvation; it is moreover one of the channels through which Christ, and certain of the blessings of His redemption, are conveyed to such participants. By feeding on Christ in this sacrament, they receive Him into their very souls. His love warms them, His peace satisfies them, His joy gladdens them, the blessed hope of glory by Him animates and strengthens them. They enter into closer sympathy with Him, they learn more of Him who is meek and lowly in heart, and get rest to their souls. They share the spirit by which He overcame the world, and triumphed over all the powers of darkness. Often, in this sacrament, they seem to sit with Christ in heavenly places, and to enjoy the choicest repasts of the heavenly banquet. Their nature, as it were, is steeped in Christ's Spirit; the old man shrivels and dies, the new nature of holiness gets fresh encouragement and support. Yet let it not be supposed for a moment that in producing such effects, the sacrament of the Supper operates like a charm. Whatever effects it may produce are brought through the action of the spiritual faculties of the soul, and especially of its great organ of appropriation—Faith. If the question were asked, What makes the sacrament of the Supper productive of higher good to an earnest Christian than a powerful sermon on the death of Christ and its saving fruits? our first answer would be, that this is due to the Holy Ghost working more powerfully through the sacrament than through the sermon; but if it should be further asked whether there be anything in the nature of the Lord's Supper to invite the more powerful action of the Holy Ghost, we should reply: 1st, that God may deem it right to put peculiar honour on an ordinance which is specially designed to show the glory of His grace in Jesus Christ, and to nourish the souls of the needy; and 2nd, that the mental preparation undergone by a careful Christian before going to the Supper—his self-examination,—his fervent prayer,—the solemnized atmosphere, so to speak,—the sympathy of his fellow-communicants,—the effort to stir up his soul to unusually strong acts of faith and love and holy desire,—the spirit of watchfulness against worldly and distracting thoughts,—his more intense resolution to banish the world from his mind, and occupy himself exclusively with his holy fellowship—that all such things as these—the usual concomitants of the Supper,—may make it a peculiarly suitable channel for the communication of extraordinary grace and blessing. Add to this, that it is of the very nature of a sacrament to call in the aid of the senses, and thus make the bodily organs a help to the faculties of the soul. When truth is *preached,* the ear alone of the bodily organs is employed to convey it to the mind; when exhibited in a sacrament, the eye, which has far more command over the mind than the ear, is also called into operation. Suppose, however, that all the accompaniments of a communion now referred to are neglected by a believer; in such a case, believer though he be, it is certain that the ordinance will convey to him but a scanty measure of grace. Even the Lord's Supper may be but as an empty well; while in proportion to the pains taken to enter into the spirit of the service and enjoy the working of the Holy Spirit, will be the degree of enjoyment and of benefit which it brings. He who rushes on this holy ground without taking the shoes from his feet—without any effort to be impressed by the sacred Presence, can only leave that Presence as he came into it; the sacrament will not be to him, as Bethel was to Jacob, the house of God or the gate of heaven.

In a word, if a sacrament is more efficacious of spiritual good than a sermon, it is not because a different kind of influence is at work, but the same influence in a higher degree. In both cases, whatever saving good takes place is due to the action of God's Spirit on the faculties of the soul.

How is the preaching of the word ever effectual? Not merely because the arguments are convincing, the illustrations clear, and the appeals forcible and appropriate; but because the Spirit opens the hearts of hearers, causes them to ponder, to feel, to tremble; and makes the truths which they have heard to live and abide in them for ever. And why are sacraments ever effectual? Not merely because in their own nature they are fitted to gender a solemn state of heart, and to direct the mind powerfully to the great doctrines of the cross; but because the Holy Spirit prepares and opens hearts to appreciate and feel the truths which they exhibit, and thus makes them channels of saving grace to the soul.

We are well aware of the pious horror which this view of the efficacy of the sacraments would raise in certain minds. Those who elevate the sacraments far above all other ordinances of the Gospel; who represent them as the most wonderful, the most mysterious, the most certain depositories of saving grace; who think that for any one to partake of a sacrament is equivalent to drinking the elixir of immortality or bathing in the River of Life; who maintain that if one do but receive the sacraments devoutly, and is but wrapt in wonder at the unapproachable privilege which is given him through God's priest, no other exercise of mind is needed for realizing the unspeakable treasure—all such persons will recoil from the view we have presented as a sacrilegious robbery, as an impious stripping the most holy mysteries of our religion of the surpassing glory with which God has invested them. But no such representation can invalidate the substantial soundness of the view we have presented. And if it should be proposed to test the question by results, we should not dread the decision. Against the excited wonder and ecstasy of Sacramentarians, we would confidently place the experience of intelligent and well-exercised Protestants. In the feelings of the former we believe there is really nothing to compare with the experience of the latter—the sense they have at the Lord's Supper of the reality and sufficiency of redemption, of the grace of the Son, the love of the Father, and the quickening power of the Holy Spirit; their lessed repose of soul in the thought of a completed and appropriated redemption; their tranquil composure and satisfaction of heart, in the belief that all that concerns them is in the hands of a covenant God; the brotherly and loving spirit which flows out to their brethren of mankind; the happy, confiding feeling with which, in the view of the past, they can contemplate the future—' Surely goodness and mercy shall follow me all the days of my life; and I will dwell in the house of the Lord for ever.'

4. We add another feature of the Christian sacraments—they are badges of Christian discipleship. He who receives them puts on, as it were, the livery of the cross. He makes a declaration before the world like Joshua's, 'As for me and my house, we will serve the Lord.' And this is not true merely in a general sense. He must be regarded moreover as making a special

profession corresponding to the character of the sacrament itself. Has he been baptized? Not only in the general does he profess himself to be Christ's, but more especially he testifies that he believes his nature to be polluted and that that nature requires to be changed. Has he been baptized into the name of the Father, Son, and Holy Ghost? Not only does he signify his belief in the Trinity, but he professes to take each of the three persons in the capacity or office specially assigned to him: the Father as his God and Portion, his Judge and Ruler; the Son as his Redeemer, his Guide, his Teacher; the Holy Spirit as his Quickener, his Comforter, his Sanctifier. Has he gone to the Holy Supper? Not only has he signified his belief in Christ and His redemption, but he has professed to appropriate Christ spiritually, and from His broken body and shed blood to draw, by faith, the blessings of reconciliation. He has declared his conviction, that if one died for all, then were all dead; and that He died that they that live should not live unto themselves, but unto Him that died for them and that rose again.

Alas, what an amount of miserable hypocrisy is often connected with these glorious sacraments! How marvellously man often contrives to reverse the tendency of Divine institutions, to pervert them to the very opposite purpose to that for which they were graciously designed! These holy ordinances, designed among other things as badges of manly profession, of free, frank, fearless appropriation of Christ, how miserably they are often perverted to the purpose of a hollow acknowledgment, used like the kiss of Judas, not to honour but betray the Son of Man! Happily we have outlived the time when these hallowed institutions were made by law the porch to every civil office and employment, and a wholesale profanation of them (as it often turned out) was carried on by the highest authorities of the land. But what has ceased to be demanded by public law is in some circles still required by the force of social custom. In nothing is the want of deep personal sincerity so often shown as in the spirit in which men receive the Christian sacraments. And in regard to the Lord's Supper, it is quite marvellous how that which was designed as a bond of union among all Christians is perverted to a badge of separation! The communion of the Lord's body and blood often becomes the crowning badge of sectarianism, in place of the holy symbol of the common faith and hope of Christians. Happily there are individual Christians who break through these miserable restraints of human origin, and delight to communicate with all of every name that love the Lord and look for His appearing. May God hasten the time when on a wider scale this most Christian spirit shall come into operation; and when, in the various Christian denominations, the one bread and the one cup which were designed to show the world the unity of the Christian Church, shall be restored to the glorious use for which they were designed! Morning star of the millennial day, arise and shine! For surely the Bridegroom's chariot will not be far off, when His people, over the memorials of His death, whatever their differences may have been before, shall be unable to know any feeling but love. Is it right that the graves of our children should have more power to bring hearts together than the feast that commemorates the death of our Lord? The poet says touchingly,

> 'For when we came where lies the child
>   We lost in other years,
> There above the little grave,
> O there above the little grave,
>   We kiss'd again with tears.

Would that the Holy Supper were such a scene:—a place where Ephraim who has so long envied Judah, and Judah who has so long vexed Ephraim, would meet to bury their quarrels and 'kiss again with tears'!

THE END.

www.ingramcontent.com/pod-product-compliance
Lightning Source LLC
Chambersburg PA
CBHW032354230426
43672CB00007B/697